A SUSSEX GUIDE

OLD-FASHIONED
FAMILY DAYS OUT
IN SUSSEX

SUSAN & GINA JAMIESON

INTRODUCED BY
JANE HISSEY

Illustrated by
SHARON SCOTLAND

SNAKE RIVER PRESS

SNAKE RIVER PRESS

Book No 19
Books about Sussex for the enthusiast

Published in 2009 by
SNAKE RIVER PRESS
South Downs Way, Alfriston, Sussex BN26 5XW
www.snakeriverpress.co.uk

ISBN 978-1-906022-18-1

This book was conceived, designed and produced by
SNAKE RIVER PRESS

ART DIRECTOR & PUBLISHER *Peter Bridgewater*
EDITORIAL DIRECTOR *Viv Croot*
EDITOR *Robert Yarham*
PAGE MAKEUP *Richard Constable & Chris Morris*
ILLUSTRATOR *Sharon Scotland*
CONSULTANT *Lorraine Harrison*

This book is typeset in Perpetua & Gill Sans,
two fonts designed by Eric Gill

Printed and bound in China

DEDICATION

to Clarice, my mother,
who showed me how to enjoy life

CONTENTS

FOREWORD

If you think back you can probably remember, with extraordinary clarity, almost every outing you went on as a child, especially, it seems, outings that involved the whole family. I wish this book had been available when my children were little. I have lived in Sussex for more than 35 years and still find that I have not visited all the places included here. I would have so enjoyed having the planning part done for me.

Children are not naturally lazy; they have laziness thrust upon them! They want to run and jump, to roll down hills and fly kites, to play hide-and-seek and explore new surroundings. When we were children we were more or less free to roam. And we did. Nowadays, it is much harder to give children that freedom to explore; to equip themselves with the skills they need to live full, adventurous, inquisitive lives. Going out for the day with children can become prohibitively expensive so it's a joy to discover that there are many exciting outings you can undertake for only the cost of the travel and a picnic.

I first met Susan Jamieson on the day we both arrived at the art college in Brighton as teenagers! We have been close friends ever since and our children have grown up together. Susan and her daughter Gina have given this book their own creative, fun-loving but supremely practical approach. It not only has ideas of where to go but what you could do while there, what to take with you and even a recipe or two for the picnic.

I have been writing and illustrating for children for the last 25 years and many of the places in this book have been the inspiration behind my books and stories for television. With my own children and the children of friends we have tramped through woods, gathered flotsam and jetsam on beaches, cycled along disused railways and picked blackberries in country lanes. Sussex is rich in destinations that fire the imagination and stimulate creativity; this book is your key to getting out there!

JANE HISSEY

INTRODUCTION

'Childhood is measured out by sounds and smells and sights,
before the dark hour of reason grows.'

JOHN BETJEMAN, 1960

I was so pleased to be asked to write this book, to share my enthusiasm for exploring the beautiful county of Sussex, in the company of family and friends, and hopefully not spending too much money on the way.

I find that the more we get out and about, the more there is to see. Our lives have become so busy we forget to say, 'Come on, let's go out for the day.' It takes some effort – getting prepared, organising a picnic, changes of clothes, maps, prising resentful folk from their computers. It can seem too much bother so we give in and go to the supermarket, catch up on the cleaning, nag about homework. But it is worth it. Days out as a family and with friends stick in the memory, and form part of our history. Children get to see their usually preoccupied parents laughing and joking. We tend to have high expectations of holidays, but days out are not so pressured, and if they don't turn out to be as exciting as we'd hoped, at least we'll be home for tea!

In my work with young children, some things stand out: they love being outside and they appreciate having the day-to-day pressures lifted. They are dashed off to nursery, to 'soft rooms', to contrived environments where the adventure is done for them. These venues have their place, but making their own adventures gives a feeling of autonomy and satisfaction, and encourages a spirit of independence.

When I was expecting my son, my lovely Doctor Caroline said, 'Oh, you'll have so much fun,' in answer to my doubts about how I would cope. She was right! And often that fun happened when we were out and about, often with friends, feeling the benefits of fresh air and a change of scene. When the babies are tiny, an outing is usually most beneficial to the mums. I remember one day being collected by a friend whose baby was born the same weekend as mine. I piled out of the house with car seat, changing bag, buggy and baby. I was in awe of her arriving approximately when she had promised, and she congratulated me on actually getting my lipstick on! We didn't go far, just a restorative walk in Stanmer Woods, but to us it was a triumph, our month-old babies sleeping as we strolled and talked and adjusted to our new lives.

My son turned out to be a very energetic boy who preferred to spend most of his time out of doors, and I often turned our small garden into an obstacle course, balancing bamboo canes on plant pots to jump over and wriggle under, using cardboard tubes to shoot cars into the laundry basket and throw balls into a box. However, he really loved to roam and explore, and we discovered the joys of mooching on the beach or climbing trees in the woods, racing his tricycle along the seafront and looking at dinosaur bones in our local museum. Money was tight, and although we enjoyed a day out at a theme park, children's farm or leisure centre, necessity caused us to seek out destinations without entrance fees.

I grew up in the Midlands, and my mother took me to the local museums, where I learned about the history of local industries. I shuddered at the models of people operating knitting machines in tiny, dark reconstructions of terraced houses, I hurried by a vast dinosaur skeleton that had been found locally, and listened as my gently curious mother asked the curator what a particularly abstract painting was 'meant to be'. These visits inspired my life-long love of museums, whether they house priceless collections, or small idiosyncratic local displays. And often they are free and child friendly, so you can pop in for a quick fix of your favourite gallery without it becoming a 'big thing'.

While researching this book I was amazed at how much there was to do in Sussex, without needing to spend more than the bus fare or car park fee. And everywhere I went, with my 14-year-old daughter Gina at my side, pointing out things she enjoyed or found interesting, we asked people what they would recommend about a particular place. They were so enthusiastic, pointing out an especially muddy walk, or a good area of beach for shells.

There are many more wonderful destinations than this book can cover, so I am sorry if I have missed out your favourites. The extensive Worthing beaches, the beautiful flower-bedecked seafront at Eastbourne,

Shoreham Airport to watch planes come and go, the highly recommended Ashdown Forest Way cycle track, Stanmer Woods, Jack and Jill Windmills, there really is so much to see.

Being out and about can encourage childrens' 'looking' skills and visual awareness. They are usually naturally good at this, but you can extend and encourage them by planning your trip ahead. The computer and internet make it easy to glean some information before you go, such as tide times, relevant history and, most important, the weather forecast. If there is a story or activity you can link in to a visit, so much the better: a honey cake in Winnie-the-Pooh country, a Kipling story for Rottingdean can all help to make your outing even more memorable.

When you visit a museum, check out the themes of the galleries beforehand. It is a shame to trek through displays that don't really grab your child's interest, when you could have gone straight to the collection of fearsome tribal masks that would have hit the button and inspired some creativity back at home. Do read some of the information about the displays, it can greatly add to everyone's enjoyment. Gina and I watched families gallop through the fascinating Hastings Fishermen's Museum, thereby missing stories of the brave and occasionally eccentric folk of the Strade. Too slow a pace will lose your audience, but excitingly narrated information brings history to life.

With younger children it is worth travelling with the odd treat or surprise in your backpack, to use as prizes or gentle bribes. The little waterproofs that pack into their own pockets are invaluable, as are foot wear appropriate to the weather and destination, wet wipes and a kitchen roll (tougher than tissues). Hats and caps all round, sunscreen, and as my gran used to say 'a nice warm woolly,' or fleece. Maps can be very helpful: once, armed with an inadequate one, we managed to get lost on the Downs, where an Ordinance Survey map would have helped us get back on track before the children started wondering how long they could survive on blackberries. Remember a camera, too, for the every-one to use. Photos of our son and his friends pretending to be sleeping lions on high branches, are an instant route back to the milestone day out we had just before they all started secondary school.

In this book some excursions are more suited to older children, and the able bodied. Others are ideal for toddlers. Most can be adapted – walks and cycle rides shortened or lengthened – and in many cases I have suggested an undercover venue as an alternative for when it rains. Gina has been an invaluable companion, observant, calm and able to remind me of our many lovely days out with her older brother. He is now 19, but still says, 'Chanctonbury Ring – amazing!' I hope you will be inspired to gather up grannies, grandpas, friends and children of all ages, to explore and have fun in Sussex, however tight your budget.

SUSAN JAMIESON

GINA SAYS

" *Writing this book with my lovely Mum has been so much fun. It was fantastic to revisit momentarily forgotten places and, as we did, memories of good times kept on springing to my mind. Distant memories of rolling down sandbanks with my big brother, or peering up as he fearlessly (as he seemed to me to be at the time!) scrambled higher and higher up the branches of trees, and lazy summer days playing rounders with my cousins, while being mooed at by disgruntled cows. Prickly blackberry bushes, scarves, hats, coats, gloves and Wellington boots, massive broken umbrellas and being buffeted by howling winds on the very top of the South Downs – all images and experiences that bring my early years flooding back into my mind.*

I have really enjoyed being involved in this book, and I do hope some of those teenagers out there, who may feel a little reluctant to venture out of the house with the rest of the family, will take a couple of days to enjoy our Sussex. "

ASHDOWN FOREST

POOH'S ENCHANTED PLACE

Ashdown Forest has a very particular landscape, quite different to that of the chalk downlands of Sussex. The forest is open heathland, with wooded areas, in the High Weald. There are sites of early ironworks, a Bronze Age tumulus known as Peat Lump Hill, evidence of two Roman roads, Garden Hill where excavations revealed a Roman villa with bath house, and many, many deer.

Ashdown Forest was enclosed as a Royal Hunting Park in the 13th century. King Edward II, born in 1284, hunted deer in the forest until his wife, Queen Isabella, and his nobles organised a revolt, and he was forced to hand over his crown to his son, Edward III, in 1327. But for many of us, the most celebrated and beloved inhabitant of Ashdown Forest is Winnie-the-Pooh. What could be jollier, on a fine day, than a picnic in 'Pooh Country', with a group of young bear enthusiasts.

We like to take Honey Cake and honey sandwiches, so if Pooh should appear he can share our picnic. Before your 'expotition', do read some Winnie-the-Pooh stories together, especially the Poohsticks one, and 'Piglet Meets a Heffalump', and remember to take the book with you, for reading *in situ*. The stories are laugh-out-loud funny, especially if you do all the voices.

The author A. A. Milne published *Winnie-the-Pooh* in 1926, with illustrations by E. H. Shepard. The characters in the books were toys belonging to Milne's son, Christopher Robin, except Pooh, who was modelled on 'Growler', a bear owned by Shepard. In his autobiography Christopher Milne wrote, 'Pooh's forest and Ashdown Forest are identical. Several places in the stories can be identified and explored.'

As the forest is huge, consult a good map and decide where you want to go. Our perfect day would start with a game of Poohsticks, on the very bridge used by Christopher Robin and Pooh. There are various information points, in particular Ashdown Forest Centre, on Coleman's Hatch Road, and the Llama Park at Wych Cross, which also has a café, shop and toilets. You can pick up maps of the walks to various Pooh-related sites, and at the Pooh Corner Shop in Hartfield buy a map specifically showing the route to Poohsticks Bridge, which is very helpful.

As we explore the forest we are always amazed at how the landscape conjures up the magical world drawn by Ernest Shepard. It is apparent that he really drew 'from life'. It is so exciting to see a place and say, 'I know that!'

Poohsticks Bridge

From the B2026 take the tiny road to Marsh Green and Newbridge. The car park is on your right. You need sensible shoes, as the round trip will take about an hour, downhill there, uphill back. Take the path leading from the car park, and enjoy collecting lots of sticks on the way. This is important because the area around the bridge has no sticks left at all.

Quite soon the path joins a road for a short distance, so be careful of traffic. Turn right by a house with two splendid horse sculptures on the gateposts. The path goes downhill, with paddocks on the left, and more handsome horses, real this time.

Suddenly the path widens, by a magnificent oak tree, and there it is, the wooden bridge so familiar from the story. It is a very peaceful scene, with the sound of trickling water and sunlight glinting on the swirling pools, but then the peace is shattered by voices young and old, urging and cheering their sticks on.

It is fun to stand in a row along the bridge, sticks held out over the water, and on the count of three, let go! Dash to the other side to watch them emerge, some will whiz out, only to run aground, others seem to

HONEY CAKE

This is our Honey Cake recipe to make at home with the children. Honey sandwiches are also something even preschoolers can attempt, using softened butter, a blunt knife and a bit of help. Remember to pack hand wipes! Honey acts as glue.

WHAT YOU NEED

- 6 oz / 175 g clear honey
- 5 oz / 150 g butter
- 3 oz / 85 g light muscovado sugar
- water
- 2 eggs, beaten
- 7 oz / 200 g self-raising flour

FOR THE ICING
- 2oz / 55g icing sugar
- 1 tbsp clear honey
- hot water

1. Preheat oven to gas mark 4/ 350° F. Cover the bottom of a greased 7-in/18-cm cake tin with rice paper. Put the honey, butter and muscovado sugar into a large pan, with a tablespoon of water and heat slowly until melted.

2. Remove from the heat and mix in the eggs and flour. Spoon the mixture into the cake tin and bake for 40-45 minutes. The cake should be springy to the touch and have shrunk a bit from the sides of the tin. Let it cool for a while before turning out on to a wire rack.

3. While the cake is cooling, sieve the icing sugar and mix with the honey and 2-3 teaspoons of hot water. Drizzle over the cake.

navigate a way through and disappear from view downstream. To avoid ownership disputes, know your stick. Pooh first played this game by accident, having tripped and dropped a fir cone. Don't forget your camera. It is great to have a photo taken holding your sticks, or fir cones if you have brought some with you, on this famous bridge.

'Perfect for a Piknick'

A little further along the B2026 from Hartfield are several more car parks. Because of our fondness for the character, we like to use the one marked 'Piglets'. Walk a short distance up a sandy path leading from the back of the car park, turn left up a short, steep incline, and on the right is 'Pooh's Enchanted Place'. On a clear day the view will take your breath away.

On the site of an Iron-Age fort, in a clearing within a semi-circle of fir trees, a bronze plaque is set into a great rock. It commemorates Milne and Shepard, who 'captured the magic of Ashdown Forest and gave it to the world'. It also says, 'and by and by they came to an enchanted place at the very top of the forest called Galleons Lap (Gills Lap). This special place looks over the Weald, the forest, and a distant patchwork of fields. It is very beautiful, and perfect for a "Piknick".' So spread out the blankets, arrange the teddy bears, and tuck in.

Walk a little further up the track, and past a large sandy pit. Could it be Roo's sandpit? And up to Gills Lap (Galleons Lap), the highest point in the forest, and a group of splendid fir trees planted closely together, with wonderfully springy turf underfoot. A fine setting for a game of hide-and-seek, or tag, with a hand on a trunk being home.

You almost feels the very air is different here. Perhaps it is the unmistakeable scent of the bracken, the soft-coloured heathers, the pop of gorse in summer. In this small area are networks of undulating sandy paths which invite exploration, and give life to the wonderful stories of Winnie-the-Pooh and his friends and relations.

GINA SAYS

"A really fun game we made up in Ashdown Forest when I was younger is one we call Heffalump Hunt. Choose the scariest person in your family to be the Heffalump, and give everybody else a character from the Winnie-the-Pooh stories. I was always Piglet! Everybody else counts to 20 very loudly as the Heffalump stumps off along the path away from the rest of the group. Then we follow the Heffalump, freezing whenever he turns around. You're out if he catches you moving. The sneakiest, most careful person will not move even the tiniest bit when the Heffalump turns around to look at them, and will eventually be so close behind him that they can catch him before he turns around. They win. The game is best when the Heffalump is really scary and growls, because then a lot of giggling is involved!"

Getting there   National grid ref. TQ479359
❱ Bus: 291 to Hartfield from Crawley and Tunbridge Wells.
  54 to Ashdown Forest from Eastbourne, Uckfield or East Grinstead.
❱ Useful website: www.ashdownforest.org, tel. 01342 823583.

BALCOMBE VIADUCT

A VICTORIAN PICNIC

The Viaduct is a truly spectacular piece of architecture, hidden away in a quiet and beautiful part of Sussex, yet easy to reach by car and close to Haywards Heath. I have loved the views up and down the Ouse Valley from the Brighton train for so many years, and sometimes, when the sun was low, could see a great shadow of the arches, far below the fields. I was delighted, therefore, when a friend told me it was possible to get right up to it, and even stand under the arches.

To find the little footpath that leads to the viaduct, drive along Bordehill Lane (very minor country road which links Balcombe and Haywards Heath). About half way along, as the road bends and dips, the viaduct suddenly appears, striding across the valley. Look out for a little pull-in, hardly a lay-by, just before a humpback bridge sign. Stop there, and cross over to a stile, with the footpath marked 'WSCC Ouse Valley Way.' Then it is a very short walk uphill through a field to the viaduct.

The setting is so grand, and genuinely Victorian, that it could be the time to really pull out all the stops for a magnificent picnic. Queen Victoria was very fond of picnics, and to go on one must have been a welcome relief from all the formality and etiquette that governed many Victorian lives. To set out on such an outing, albeit with servants to carry the furniture and food, would have been rather liberating.

The ground around the viaduct is definitely not manicured grass, so you could do the whole Victorian thing and take camping tables and chairs, with cloths and cutlery, and even, as some Americans do, wear period costume! We tend to have a Spartan approach to eating out of doors, but Gina always enjoys the fact that even at motorway lay-bys in France, the French spread out a pretty cloth on the grubby picnic tables. How posh!

It is interesting to note (to me, anyway) that men were required to do much of the work at a Victorian picnic, not just carrying and serving, but also they were expected to be delightful and entertaining! Apparently they were not even allowed to sit down until invited.

A proper spread

Some picnic health and safety. Keep cold food chilled, especially poultry, fish, meat, mayonnaise, butter, cream and cheese. Mrs Beeton didn't worry about packing everything into a coolbox though, and wrote in the 1850s that an appropriate bill of fare, for a picnic of 40 people, should consist of 'a joint of cold roast beef, a joint of cold boiled beef, 2 ribs of lamb, 2 shoulders of lamb, 4 roast fowls, 2 roast ducks, 1 ham, 2 veal pies, 2 pigeon pies, 6 medium lobsters, 1 piece of collard calf's head, 18 lettuces, 6 baskets of bread and 6 cucumbers'! Pudding was equally elaborate with blancmanges and many other things made in moulds. The whole repast ended with tea made in a portable stove.

I'm not suggesting doing a Mrs Beeton, but sometimes it can be worth making a bit of a 'do': pasties, perhaps, prepared the day before and cooked just before setting off, still delicious when cooled. It is easy to make both vegetarian and meat fillings, and encourage children to decorate them with pastry flowers and leaves. Packed into a shallow baking tray, loosely covered with foil or greaseproof paper, they travel well. Add a large green salad, with dressing carried separately in screw top jar, and pickles, chutneys, some cheese, butter and a rustic loaf.

Some home-made lavender lemonade would be appropriate for a summer picnic, as it is so refreshing and fragrant, and can be made the night before and transported in mineral water bottles. For pudding, strawberries, raspberries, cream and home-made shortbread are hard to beat. (Mrs Beeton would probably have preferred jellies and suchlike in elaborate moulds to have a place on the picnic cloth.) Our family loves old-fashioned trifle, but it has to be well set to travel. Victorians would have expected good china and cutlery too, but plastic tableware is now so attractive I think it will do. I don't care too much for plastic knives and forks though. We take the real thing, and a corkscrew.

This outing is not really recommended for very young children, they are too small to climb up the arches, and the ground around has lots of nettles and briars and a trickling stream, that is, apparently, the River Ouse, over which the viaduct was built. Older children, however, will have a great time clambering up into the bases of the huge arches. Remember to take some balls and rackets, for a game of archway 'tennis'.

Railway grandeur

It is impossible to be unmoved by such an extraordinary structure. The viaduct was built to extend the train line to Brighton, and was completed in 1842. It is Grade II listed, and underwent restoration ten years or so ago. It has carried trains for almost 170 years, and is testimony to the skill of architect David Mocatta, engineer John Urpeth Rastrick, and over 5,000 labourers who worked for four years, digging cuttings, building bridges and hewing tunnels.

There are 37 graceful arches supporting the railway above. The viaduct is nearly 98 feet (30 metres) high, and each arch has an immense 'hole' through it, so you can stand at one end and look through to the end walls. The 11 million bricks were brought from Holland, via Newhaven, up the Ouse by barge.

LAVENDER LEMONADE

WHAT YOU NEED

- 5 cups of water
- 1½ cups of granulated sugar
- ¼ cup lavender leaves, chopped
- 1 cup freshly squeezed lemon juice

1. Heat half of the water, add the sugar and boil until it is dissolved.

2. Add the lavender leaves and allow to cool at room temperature. Strain out the leaves. Decant into a jug and add the lemon juice and the remaining water. Stir and taste, adding more sugar if necessary.

3. Chill before pouring into clean bottles.

After your fine Victorian picnic, continue the theme and play some old-fashioned games, such as tag. Lively children will just be itching to climb in and out of the arches. In fact my son and a friend took their picnic and ate it sitting up in an arch some distance away! While the adults chat over a cup of tea, noisy games of catch or tennis through the arches can take place. The visual effect of millions of bricks going off into the distance is very strange, rather like a print by Escher. Take cameras, as creative children will find many photo opportunities. Even our dog was hauled up into an arch to have her photograph taken. The trains pass overhead frequently (110 of them a day), but such is the solidity of the structure you can only hear a gentle hum.

When the picnic has run its course, the food eaten and the gentlemen's inclination to be delightful has waned, pack everything back in the car and take a walk. Follow the path beyond the viaduct, over two more very high styles and into a field, which enables you to see the viaduct crossing the valley, and the trains whizzing by. On our last visit it was very damp under the arches, so we carried our picnic up here and ate it on a handy log, watching and waving at the trains.

Should you prefer just a walk to look at the viaduct, and a picnic elsewhere, there is the appropriately named Victoria Park, in nearby Haywards Heath. It is suitable for all ages, with a children's playground and paddling pool, beautiful trees for shade, handy goalposts, and even a skateboard and BMX park.

GINA SAYS

"Get your friends to pose (if they're anything like mine you won't have much trouble doing this!). Any photo opportunity is bound to be the highlight of the day!) in one of the big holes cut out of the arches. It makes a great picture.

I can't help feeling as if I'm in a modern day version of The Railway Children, *sitting on the grass watching and waiting for the trains zooming by."*

Getting there   National grid ref. TQ312291

❯ Car: from Haywards Heath drive north along Balcombe Road,
  which becomes Bordehill Lane; from Balcombe drive south along Haywards Heath Road,
  which does the same.

BEACHY HEAD

LIGHTHOUSES & LIFEBOATS

The South Downs just west of Eastbourne have a wild, sweeping beauty, which undulates all the way to Rottingdean. On a clear and sunny day the combination of jewel bright grass, white cliffs and azure sea is exhilarating. However, the cliff paths are not suitable for young, free-range children, or unleashed dogs, because the cliff edge is mostly unfenced and the drop down to the seashore is 551 feet (168 metres) in places!

There are two lighthouses for the price of one here: the Belle Tout and the Beachy Head. The distinctive red and white striped Beachy Head lighthouse is very impressive whether seen from the vertiginous cliffs above, or from down on the beach. If you decide to take the beach route, it is vital to check the tide times. It would be easy to become stranded, so make sure the tide is going out when you set off, leaving plenty of time for your return trip.

Walk down to the beach at the extreme western end of Eastbourne, signposted Holywell. There is a café and, provided the tide is going out, lots of rockpools and sand. My children have always loved climbing on the weathered wooden groynes, hauling each other up and jumping down the other side on to lovely sand. Continue along the beach west-wards, keeping well away from the cliffs, which are very crumbly.

From this beach, called Falling Sands, you can see the lighthouse, dwarfed by the mighty cliffs above. In the early 18th century a local vicar, Parson Jonathan Darby, became distressed at having to bury so many poor sailors drowned when their ships were wrecked on this coast. So he decided to do something about it. He enlarged caverns in the cliff, above high water mark, and lit fires in them to warn the ships that they were near to land and should steer away. On stormy nights he would keep the lights burning, having been lowered down by his parishoners. Sometimes, when the ferocious south-westerly gales drove the ships on to the rocks, the sailors could be pulled to safety in 'Parson Darby's Hole'. He was buried in Friston churchyard in 1726, and his epitaph reads: 'He was the sailor's friend'. After his death, smugglers took over the cave to hide their contraband, which seems a very sad end for such a noble venture. And of course, without the warning light, ships were again wrecked.

Eventually, in the early 19th century, after a trading vessel ran aground (the crew were saved), the government was asked to take action to protect its ships. Belle Tout lighthouse was the result, built high up on the cliff top near to Beachy Head, first as a wooden structure, then a more permanent stone tower. It was partly financed by wealthy eccentric John 'Mad Jack' Fuller. The lamp was lit in 1834 and was finally extinguished in 1902 because fog, which often occurs here, obscured the light to boats out at sea. This led to the building of the Beachy Head lighthouse down in the sea, as the light would be enhanced by the water and white cliffs behind. The Belle Tout lighthouse had a media moment for a while in 1999 when it was moved on rollers away from the crumbling cliff edge.

If you are taking young school-age children to see the Beachy Head lighthouse I would really recommend reading some of Ronda and David Armitage's stories about Mr Grinling the Lighthouse Keeper before you go. The adventures of the endearing lighthouse keeper and his long suffering wife and cat, take place around a splendid red and white lighthouse, just like this one. Mr Grinling has a very keen interest in food, and his picnic will inspire you to great things!

On the beach, keep a close lookout for fossils. The chalk cliffs here are constantly eroding and when the tide goes out, it can leave behind treasures such as ammonites on the foreshore.

Another way to view the lighthouse is by following the pleasingly named Peace Path. It is easily accessible from the Eastbourne to Birling Gap road. Cross the road, carefully, and join the wheelchair friendly path opposite the toilets in the car park. This is a circular walk on a well-surfaced path that gives spectacular views on a clear day. As you walk towards the cliff edge you definitely get a seagull's perspective, and my husband says the sheer drop makes him 'peculiar'. There is a viewing area (with barriers) and to the east the views extend over the Eastbourne skyline to Hastings and even to Dungeness power station over 30 miles (48 km) away. Look west, and far down below, beneath the towering cliffs, is the lighthouse. The line of the Downs leads the eye past Belle Tout lighthouse towards Selsey Bill in the far west of the county. When the tide is out you can see the platform created by the erosion of the cliffs which is caused by the waves battering the chalk. In 1999 there was a huge rock fall behind the lighthouse, so keep away from the edge.

The lighthouse was completed in 1902, and was powered by paraffin. It was a tremendous feat of construction, using a cableway from the top of the cliffs to carry materials, including 3,660 tons of Cornish granite, down to sea level. Now fully automated, the flash can be seen for 25 miles (40 km) out to sea. As you follow the path round look out for the many lovely downland butterflies. Even with many visitors, Beachy Head is a strange and evocative place, poised so very high above the sea.

A downland experience

Back across the road you come to the Countryside Centre. Housed in what was a signalman's cottage, built by Lloyds of London for shipping reports, it has a shop and various displays in 'The Downland Experience'. As you enter there is a scale model of the Beachy Head lighthouse, which will flash its light at you for 10 pence. A panel of photographs portrays the work of PC Harry Ward, who patrolled this area for 13 years. He rode the clifftop on horseback, first on Princess Patricia, then Jumbo. He made more than 30 descents over the cliff edge to retrieve people, whether alive, injured or dead, who had slipped over. He even rescued dogs, so remember to keep yours on a lead by the cliffs.

The formation of the chalk cliffs is explained: they are the creation of the shells of billions of minute creatures which fell to the bottom of the sub-tropical sea. Later upheavals raised the seabed to surface level. There is a reconstructed Bronze Age hut, based on excavated evidence in the Ouse Valley. Considering it is a depiction of times so long ago it seems quite a sophisticated life, with weaving, pottery and a grain store, all protected by wattle and daub walls and a thatched roof.

There are feely boxes, which Gina and I can't bring ourselves to try, and an attractive reconstruction of a chalk cliff, complete with birds and nests, and buttons to press to hear the bird calls. Also there are lots of flint artefacts, from exquisite heart-shaped arrowheads, to rough hand axes and a hoard of Roman coins. Lift a cloth to look at a collection of beautiful downland butterflies, and shudder at the very large wasps' nest safely secured in a glass case.

Near the exit is an 'animated' figure of Walter the Shepherd, which made us jump when his face suddenly lit up (you have to see it) and he spoke. What he said was very interesting, about his life on the Downs for 84 years, earning £20 a year for looking after 400 sheep! He supplemented his income by catching little birds called wheatears, which were considered a delicacy. The name apparently derives from 'white arse' because of their plumage.

Lifeboat heroes

If you travel back into Eastbourne, you'll find the Eastbourne Lifeboat Museum on King Edward's Parade. Still on the theme of saving lives and ships at sea, do take a look in this fascinating little museum, which is also a RNLI shop. You can take a museum quiz sheet around with you. There are beautiful models of lifeboats to look at, which incited cries of delight from visiting small boys. On the walls are fine photographs of courageous lifeboat men, some wearing their medals.

The first lifeboats were rowed, and there are dramatic pictures of the rescue of a large Norwegian barge, in 1883, off Belle Tout. It took ten horses two hours to pull the lifeboat, the *William Mary*, on its carriage over the Downs to Birling Gap. The Gap was too narrow, so they had to cut away the cliffs before they could launch the boat. The crew rowed through mountainous seas in appalling conditions to reach the barge and 16 crew were successfully saved. They then had to row back, heavily laden, and pull the lifeboat back to Eastbourne!

The museum building is the William Terris Memorial Lifeboat House. It was built in memory of a famous actor, who rescued a young boy from drowning in 1887. He was awarded a medal for this gallant act. Tragically he was stabbed by a deranged fellow actor outside the Adelphi Theatre in London. He was a household name and very popular, playing many famous roles, and described as 'a friend of hundreds, with a genial, frank and winning manner'.

In 1822, following the grounding of the East Indiaman *Thames*, when six men were lost, the first Eastbourne lifeboat was funded by 'Mad Jack' Fuller, the financier of the Belle Tout. His lifeboat was credited with saving 55 lives!

GINA SAYS

"On our most recent visit to Beachy Head, it was a really beautiful, sunny day, and I noticed that the sea and the sky were such similar shades of blue that I couldn't tell where the sea stopped and the sky began! It was a bit surreal really! It does give you a bit of a slightly funny feeling altogether, being so high up above the sea and the pebbles. I have to be extra careful as well because my brother seems to find grabbing my shoulders and jerking me forward then backwards, while telling me he'd save my life, absolutely hilarious. I don't agree! Neither does my Mum. I think it makes her a bit jittery.

There's so much to see and learn in the countryside centre as well, it's really interesting, especially the bird calls section."

Getting there   National grid ref. TU588955
⊘ Bus: 12A runs daily from Brighton to Eastbourne via Beachy Head; Sunday service is 12C, mornings only. A summertime-only service runs from Eastbourne Pier to Beachy Head.
⊘ Useful website: William Terris Memorial Lifeboat House: www.eastbournernli.org.uk

BRIGHTON BEAUTIFUL

FISHING & FASHION

Brighton is on the coast, due south of London, and people have dashed to the resort since the Prince Regent made it fashionable in Regency times. The quiet fishing village of Brighthelmstone was transformed into the fashionable place to be. The railway station is just a ten-minute walk from the sea.

It is very uplifting to set off on a bright morning, heading south, downhill towards the sea. Breathing in the salty air, tinged with aromas of vinegar and chips, an almost palpable feeling of excitement grips us.

There are wonderful things to do and see all within easy walking distance. Although there are many ways to spend money in Brighton, there are also plenty of interesting, child-friendly activities and destinations which can be enjoyed for no expenditure.

Walk due south from the station, and the seafront beckons. After negotiating the busy sea-front road, there is a choice – left or right, east or west. To the west is a children's play area, with a large sandpit and paddling pool, and plenty of seating for weary adults.

The beach in Brighton is pebbly, with some sand when the tide is right out. It is a Blue Flag beach and there are lifeguards, so older or more able swimmers can enjoy sea swimming. The pebbles, however, can be very hard to walk on, so flip-flops help. In the sea stand the burnt, buckled remains of the poor old West Pier, once beautiful and now quite melancholy.

Turn east and walk along in the direction of the Palace Pier, along the lower promenade. There are souvenirs, ices, sails and sculptures, all great for a game of I-spy. Next stop is the Fishing Museum, at Arch No 201. This little museum is quite charming, and we particularly liked the name boards from old boats: *Our Ivy* and *Mary Joyce*. Were they named after someone's sweetheart or mother?

Inside there is a 27-foot (8-metre) beach boat to look at, and wonder how they got it through the door! Sea-faring memorabilia, and an audio presentation of fishing folk singing and speaking in soft Sussex accents, add to the atmosphere. Look for the pieces of ornate ironwork from the wreck of the West Pier, and photos showing how grand it once was. The arches housing the museum were used by fishermen from 1813, and still retain a damp, salty atmosphere with the particular quality of light you find in buildings connected with the sea. Outside are boats for young fishermen and pirates to climb over and sit in, and there are two traditional shellfish stalls adjacent to the museum, for a delicious kipper or mackerel roll.

Climb back up to the road level and spot two modern sculptures, one nicknamed the 'donut', the other the kissing wall. Turn back into town, up East Street, where you might see street artists and performers, and fortune-tellers, and cross over into the Royal Pavilion Gardens. This is the perfect spot to enjoy a picnic, and perhaps tea and ice creams from the open-air café, which is a Brighton institution.

Brighton Museum & Art Gallery

The entrance to this delightful and eccentric museum can now be found in the Royal Pavilion Gardens. The imposing central hall houses an impressive collection of 20th-century art and design, which really does have something to interest everyone. Can you spot a Salvador Dali sofa, shaped like a pair of lips? Or a huge leather seat in the form of a hand? At the end of the main gallery is a room aimed at children, the Discovery Room. It has illusions, and visual and literary jokes, which repay some study! Small people can climb through the fireplace, and pop their head up into a fish-tank.

My children have always been fascinated by things Egyptian, and the James Green Gallery of World Art has some thrilling exhibits. They particularly like the mummified cat with a surprised expression, the jars for preserving 'innards', and the beautifully painted but tiny sarcophagus of a very small girl. Also here are headdresses and tribal costumes from around the world, and jewellery made from teeth and bones. Gory or spine tingling exhibits usually go down well with the young.

Upstairs, in the Performance Gallery, you can get inside a Punch and Judy booth and put on a show. In the Body Gallery there are displays of tattoos, piercings, wigs and corsets, enough to interest the most jaded teenager. One display we always return to, and shudder at, are tiny and exquisite shoes once worn by Chinese women whose feet had been broken and bound, to keep them small.

In the Fashion and Style Gallery you can try on some of the garments, and we like to marvel at the enormous breeches worn by George IV in 1827, cleverly displayed to show his girth! Older members of the party will also find garments displayed similar to those we wore in the 'olden-days'! 'Why didn't you keep them?' wail the teenagers who would now love to own that Biba dress or original kaftan!

GINA SAYS

"Brighton Museum has played a really big part in my childhood – days spent wandering around gazing at its unique objects and artefacts. Parts of it are more interactive and they are fun, but I still do love the mysterious, gloomy displays that have always been there. I especially like a huge model of a smiling Galle cat, with a portrait of a dog on a pendant round its neck, the painting of a lady reading to a little girl, and the sofa shaped like lips that I would really like in my bedroom!"

Getting there   National grid ref. TQ313042

◉ Brighton is well served by excellent train services to its main station
   and by regular buses from surrounding areas.

◉ Useful website: www.brighton.virtualmuseum.info, tel. 01273 292882.

CAMBER

SAND CAKE & CASTLES

I grew up in the Midlands, far from the seaside, and the wonder of seeing the sea almost every day. Perhaps twice a year we would make the seemingly endless journey to the coast – Scarborough, Llandudno, Skegness – or, more rarely, head south. During the long intervals between holidays, sand took on an almost mystical quality, and seashells were examined and marvelled at, held firmly over our ears to try and capture that whoosh whoosh sound of the sea.

My dear aunt, a person tuned into things that made a child happy, would take me to the 'black-pad', a dismal lane behind the houses, and fill a shoe box with builder's sand that had been dumped there. We would hurry away home, the outing always accompanied by a frisson of guilt. Then I would create my own beach at home, arranging shells, pouring in water, and relive those rare, happy times by the sea. Older folks would bring home a hank of seaweed, to hang outside and consult like a barometer, 'seaweed damp, rain on the way' type of thing. I wonder if it still happens?

My aunt also had a recipe which she called Sand Cake and of course as a child I thought sand was a vital ingredient. I guess it was because the ground rice gives a slightly crisp surface, like sun-dried sand. It is a very weighty loaf type of cake, great for slicing at the beach where you don't want anything sticky. The recipe is on page 30, so why not make it with your kids for your next beach-based outing.

Camber & the castle

Camber lies at the extreme east of the county, and you can see for miles across the bay to the vast power station at Dungeness and nowadays the forest of wind farms too. The village, which has cafés and shops, shelters behind a high bank of sand dunes.

To the southwest of Rye is Camber Castle, a pleasant 1-mile (1.6-km) walk across fields, which could be inspiring for sandcastle builders. It was built by Henry VIII, completed in 1544 at the cost of £23,000, in a highly symmetrical pattern around a central single tower built previously by Sir Edmund Guldeford. The castle was in use for only about 100 years, as the silting of the Camber River made it obsolete.

Many interesting items have been found, including knives, keys, rings and buckles, even leather shoes, iron cannon balls, swords and arrowheads. The walk takes you through Rye Nature Reserve, so look out for birds, plants and insects particular to this landscape. As it was abandoned Camber Castle is still very much as it was built, and could be easily copied with round buckets at the beach.

It is fascinating to realise that the castle was once by the sea, and nearby Rye was also almost surrounded by water, and was a fishing village before the Norman Conquest. The sea has retreated almost 2 miles (3 km) leaving the town high and dry. (Don't miss a good opportunity for improvised poetry here.)

Camber Sands

Be prepared. Check the tide times, as at low tide the sea goes out an incredibly long way, leaving a vast expanse of firm, fine sand to enjoy. Bring sunglasses for everyone, as the light can be dazzling and the wind can blow fine sand into your eyes. Buckets and spades are a must. Kites respond well to the Camber breezes. My son likes to bring his skim board. If you are planning anything competitive, a few small treats are in order as prizes. Slabs of Sand Cake are very sustaining too! If we are travelling by car, we bring our own windbreak.

The long stretch of sand dunes were used as a cover by smugglers, landing goods on the beach or at Jury Gut, south of the village. In 1821

AUNTY'S SAND CAKE

WHAT YOU NEED

- *6 oz / 175 g butter*
- *6 oz / 175g) caster sugar*
- *3 eggs*
- *5 oz / 140 g self-raising flour*
- *5 oz / 125 g ground rice*
- *pinch of salt*
- *grated rind of one lemon*
- *1-2 tbsp warm lemon juice*

1. Preheat oven at gas mark 4/350°F. Line a 2lb-(900-g) tin.

2. Cream the butter and sugar. Beat in the eggs, one at a time. Stir in the flour, rice, salt, lemon rind and lemon juice. Cook for approximately 1¼ hours until golden brown.

the 'Battle of Brookland' took place between customs and excise men and the Aldington Gang, sometimes known as the Blues. One of the members, Cephas Quested, was captured and hanged after refusing to betray the gang. Eventually, in 1826, the leader Richard Morgan was arrested, charged with murder, and deported to Tasmania. Smuggling was once known as 'owling', after the owl-like noises the smugglers made to communicate with each other in the dark. By 1714, local records show that the majority of the community was involved in smuggling.

Parking is behind the dunes, and there are good facilities, including low 'foot sinks' to wash off the sand. As we like to take our family dog on outings with us, we choose car parks behind 'dogs allowed' beaches. These are clearly marked so the dog-free can just as easily avoid them.

Walk up through the sand dunes which can be quite a climb. The dunes (the only ones in Sussex) are created by sea, wind and sun. The waves grind shells and rocks into sand, the sun dries it when the tide goes out and the wind blows it inland where it collects around plants such as marram grass. The roots of the dune plants are very fragile, so everyone must take care not to damage them. Without the dunes, the village of Camber might disappear under the wind-borne sand. Plants and insects that have adapted to exist on shifting sand and withstand winds and salt are found on the dunes, as is the common lizard, although you need to be quick to catch a glimpse of one.

When you reach the top of the dunes the beach spread out before you is a very cheering sight, some 2½ miles (4 km) long, and if the tide is out, the sea's edge seems almost to be at the horizon. It would take a jaded heart not to want to charge, slithering and sliding on the fine sand, down to the beach. It could be easy to mislay your parents on such an expanse of sand, so helpfully the footpaths are numbered on large signs where they join the beach. When you have chosen your spot, look for the nearest number, and encourage everyone to remember it.

As the beach is very flat, the tide can come in and go out extremely quickly, so be aware! Look out for the warning Orange Flag, indicating an offshore wind, so no inflatables or you could end up in France (which might be nice!). Beware of buried fences and wire, and my children's favourite sign 'This is not a nudist beach, cover up'. The combination of sun and wind is very burning, so bring sun cream and hats.

Now for some serious digging. Perhaps inspired by Henry VIII, some Camber castles can be built by receding sea! The sand is a great texture for moulding and lends itself perfectly to creating sand portraits of your family and friends. This can be particularly rewarding if they have a

---

BEACH CRICKET

Anarchy is often the norm when beach cricket is played. If you have very young children, or fiercely competitive older ones (or adults) playing, then it's probably a good idea to instigate some ground rules, however flexible.

YOU NEED

- *2 bats – cricket, rounders or tennis rackets*
- *Stumps – a beach bag or upturned deck chair often serves the purpose*
- *Ball – tennis ball for safety reasons*
- *Players – any number as there are no teams, the more the merrier.*

Rule 1: choose two players by lot to bat against each other. Every one else fields. Whoever bowls a batter out becomes the new second batter. Decide a limit by time or score.

Other rules: these depend on the locale, who is playing and family traditions. For instance 'over and out' can mean 'over the sandcastle' or 'over the fence' whatever seems most appropriate. If one batter is hogging the limelight, introduce a top limit of runs so that everyone gets a go. If you are dealing with a lot of short legs, make the length they have to run shorter.

feature that stands out: a noble nose, curly hair, no front teeth. Then build up an elaborate picture frame, perhaps decorated by shells and seaweed. Keep the subject a secret until it is finished, then you can ask everyone to try and guess who it is!

The sheer size of the exposed beach invites games: frisbee, football, rounders and beach cricket all add to the fun. One year, when I was about ten, all the family found themselves on just such a beach, and even my grandma joined in with the cricket match, albeit sitting on a folding chair somewhere behind the batsman, offering boiled sweets at critical moments in the game.

Finally, but as a bonus, Camber Sands is jewelled with pretty shells. When all the digging, swimming, catching, chasing and paddling are done, you can all wander along quietly collecting these free treasures of the sea. At home, on a rainy day, get the children to wash and dry them carefully, then glue them onto little boxes and cardboard frames. When the glue has set, they can be coated with a clear varnish, and all the original delicate colours will be revealed. The results make perfect presents for friends and family.

GINA SAYS

"Didn't find a lizard to take home, but oh well, my birthday's coming up!

It's really fun messing about in the sand dunes, which by the way are much easier to get up if you run, honestly! (Mum doesn't believe me.) You don't have time to sink much. They're good for hide-and-seek, or races to the bottom (sit down at the top, push off and you'll go for miles – if you get this technique right). Sandy pants though, I'm afraid, are a definite side effect of this game, so beware!

The funniest thing is that moving fast just isn't possible in sand like this so every movement has to be in slow motion. Hide in one of the dunes and be entertained for hours watching disgruntled families struggle across the hills!"

Getting there   National grid ref. TQ9218
- Buses: Camber and Rye are both accessible by bus services.
  There is a regular connection between Camber and Rye.
- Useful websites: Camber Castle www.english-heritage.org.uk
  Camber Sands www.eastsussex.gov.uk

CHANCTONBURY RING

IF YOU DARE!

This fantastic and atmospheric walk is perhaps more suited to slightly older children. The way is steep, and can be very slippery. (After such a climb a hearty picnic is essential.) My family are always very enthusiastic about this particular outing, which is as rewarding on a crisp winter day as in high summer. Before the hurricane of 1987, the crest of the hill was crowned with a perfect copse of beech trees, originally planted by a far-sighted young Charles Goring in 1760. Before he died, aged 85, he wrote a poem about them.

How oft around thy Ring, sweet hill
A boy, I used to play
And form my plans to plant thy top
On some auspicious day

And then an almost hopeless wish
Would creep within my breast,
Oh! Could I live to see thy top
In all its beauty dress'd

That time's arrived; I've had my wish
And lived to eighty-five;
I'll thank my God who gave such grace
As long as ere I live.

Chanctonbury Ring is on the South Downs just north of Worthing. The Ring was actually a small Iron-Age hillfort, looking north over the Weald. Close by is the burial mound of a young Bronze-Age woman buried with a bronze dagger some 3,500 years ago. The hillfort was constructed 1,000 years later. After the Roman invasion, it appears that the fort was abandoned for about 300 years. Excavations where the tree roots disturbed the ground in the centre of the Ring show remains of two Roman temples, and rather excitingly, many Roman coins have been found in the area.

Because the Ring has such a commanding position, it was used in 1588 as a beacon site to warn of the approach of the Spanish Armada. Excavations have also revealed a Neolithic flint axe, Iron-Age and Romano-British pottery, and animal bones.

Ring magic

Of even more interest to my children are the legends and myths surrounding the Ring. According to some stories Chanctonbury Ring was formed, along with some other hillforts, and the Isle of Wight, by the Devil flinging great clods of earth over his shoulder as he dug out Devil's Dyke. He can be summoned to appear by running backwards seven times around the clump of trees. This format varies, some tales giving specific dates or times, such as midnight, Midsummer Eve, moonless nights, take your pick! When the Devil appears he will offer soup, milk or porridge. (I would prefer something stronger in the circumstance.) If his offer is accepted, he will take your soul in return. Some tales tell of the Ring being a haunt of fairies, who dance and cavort there on Midsummer Night's Eve.

Then there are the UFO sightings! Over the years there have been reports of a large, glowing object flying low over the trees, people experiencing sensations of extreme cold, and one man levitated up into the air for several seconds, before being dropped painfully back to the ground!

So much appears to be going on that you'll be pleasantly surprised by the peace and beauty at the summit! However, Chanctonbury is undoubtedly imbued with a contagious magical atmosphere.

Where to begin? We always start off at the car park situated in Chanctonbury Ring Road, off the A283 between Storrington and Steyning. Walk to the end of the road, and continue up the lane following the blue bridleway sign. The lane becomes a track with high banks on either side. At various stages, we have imagined ourselves to be in Alan Garner's story, *The Weirdstone of Brisingamen*, evading Svarts, or dodging Nazgul in Tolkien's *Lord of the Rings*, such is the mysterious atmosphere here.

Climb up the bank to the left and a clearing opens out, with the most spectacular tree roots exposed, like writhing serpents, down the hillside. Children love to climb through them, they form a marvellous natural adventure playground. Above the tangled web of roots, hang ropes suspended from the enormous trees overhead. We always speculate who it is that renews them, so that generations of children can dangle and swing so precariously. We wonder, are the ropes always there? It always makes me nervous to see my children, and even my husband, launch themselves out on the ropes, shrieking with fear and glee. The activity wouldn't pass any risk assessment though and you might prefer to continue straight up the track.

Return to the main track and continue upwards through the woods. Soon you have a precipitous drop to one side, a steep wall of trees to the other. This stretch can seem hard work and quite long, although there are many distracting logs to climb and interesting fungi to spot.

All of a sudden the trees clear and you come out into the light, with open fields and downland uplifting your spirits. Take the right-hand route, signed the South Downs Way. This ancient, well-trodden path goes all the way from Winchester to Eastbourne. The skies seem huge up here and, at 783 feet (239 metres), Chanctonbury is one of the highest points in West Sussex. Our Iron-Age ancestors would have had a marvellous vantage point to spot any invaders, as the views are spectacular over downland and out towards Cissbury Ring, the sea and, on a clear day, the Isle of Wight.

After passing a cattle grid, the hillfort lies ahead of you across a vast green downland field, lovely for a good run. I strongly believe our children need to stretch out and breathe in fresh air, turn cartwheels and experience being 'out of doors'. This special piece of the South Downs has a real 'on top of the world' feeling.

On arriving at Chanctonbury you will find you can't actually go into the Ring, as it has barbed wire to protect the young trees planted after the hurricane of 1987. No matter, there are lovely places to sit and picnic on the grassy banks all around. Let the prevailing wind decide where you spread out the picnic. We like to revisit a rather odd tree, like a bridge, to the north-east of the Ring, which appears to have both ends in the ground. It makes a great photo with everyone arranged underneath its arc.

It is a very peaceful place to sit and spot landmarks to the north in the Weald, while more energetic members of the party climb and explore. I'm not sure whether UFOs are ever sighted in the daytime, but it would seem that at Chanctonbury Ring anything is possible.

GINA SAYS

"*I love this day out. There are so many really fun things to do just on the way up the hill. My favourite part of the walk is the great mass of tangled tree roots that stick out of the chalk. I always climb inside and crawl around — it's really eerie!*

It's a good idea to bring a map of Sussex for when you get to the top of the hill, because then you can try to spot certain landmarks. It's really exciting to see something familiar so far below you! Also, bring your camera and go all the way round the Ring (not backwards!) taking panoramic photos, and put them all together either on your camera or at home. Looks impressive!"

Getting there   National grid ref. TQ139120

❱ Bus: no direct service but there are buses to Findon village or Washington from where it can be reached on foot, but it will involve quite a long walk.

❱ Useful website: www.findon.info/chanctonbury

CUCKMERE HAVEN

SEVEN SISTERS & A SNAKE

We often return to the Seven Sisters Country Park whose 'Snake River' route, along the meandering Cuckmere River, is particularly suited to buggies and bikes,. The path from the car park or bus stop down to the beach, is very easy walking on a good surface. In honour of the Seven Sisters, we sometimes make little buns called 'Crumbling Cliffs'; they are quick and easy, and ideal to take down to the beach at Cuckmere.

The journey to Cuckmere is particularly exciting if you take the double-decker bus, from Eastbourne or Brighton, and get off at the Seven Sisters Country Park Visitor Centre at Exceat. Begin with a look around the centre. You can pick up a Seashore Safari sheet, packed with advice, information and interesting things to look out for. The suggested activities are great fun and will soon have the whole family looking and listening and, of course, learning. Remember to pack a few pencils, as there are charts and grids to fill in too.

There are plenty of 'hands on' things for fiddly fingers to explore. More than a dozen skulls, including those of a sheep, badger and dolphin, are on display to look at, feel and compare along with examples of things to look out for on the shore: 'mermaid's purses' and shells. There is also a resin pebble with a piece of metal embedded in it. Apparently, to help plot lonmgshore drift, a metal detector was used to trace the pebble as it was moved along by the tides.

CRUMBLING CLIFF BUNS

WHAT YOU NEED

• *rice paper*
• *2 egg whites*
• *4 oz / 115g caster sugar*
• *6oz / 175g desiccated coconut*
• *angelica (for grass and cliff tops)*

1. Preheat oven at gas mark 3 / 325°F. Cover a greased baking sheet with rice paper. Whisk egg whites till very stiff (dare you turn the bowl upside down?).

2. Carefully fold in the sugar and coconut. Place spoonfuls onto the rice paper. Top with slivers of angelica for the 'grass'.

3. Bake for 15 minutes. Don't let them brown too much. Allow to cool, remove from sheet and pack carefully into plastic boxes.

Plunge your hands into the feely boxes, see a display of coastal erosion, and another of the inevitable plastic bottles, nets and other rubbish washed up on our beaches. Children are particularly horrified by these, so hopefully their generation will be committed environmentalists. I must make a point here of saying how friendly, knowledgeable and helpful are the volunteers who run the Centre.

Outside, peer into a shepherd's hut, find a trough in the shape of a dog, note the Exceat Farmhouse for a welcome cup of tea on your return. And, very important, the toilets are situated here, behind the centre, not on the beach!

Cross carefully over the busy A259 and enter the park via a wooden gate. There is a signpost indicating walks of different lengths and difficulty. Take the path to the beach and Seven Sisters, and keep following signs to the beach all the way there. Downland rises to the left, while the Cuckmere River flows peacefully on the right. This is a tidal river, so look out as you go for the many different birds that inhabit the area. We watched little egrets wading in the shallows until disturbed, when they flew off, pointing their yellow feet like airborne ballet dancers, and surprising us with their harsh cries.

Behind the beach lies a salt marsh. Plants grow here which have specially adapted to living in such salty conditions. The brackish water can be a bit pungent in places. The path will take you to the eastern end of the beach. If you are there at low tide, notice the remains of a wreck the *Polynesia*, a German sailing ship that ran aground in 1810.

Although nowadays it seems so peaceful, it wasn't always a wildlife haven. Smugglers used the beach in past centuries. During World War II the area was identified as a potential landing site for invading forces, so various obstacles and ditches were put into place. At night, lights were positioned in order to confuse bombers into thinking that they were flying over Newhaven. More recently the area has featured in the movies: *Robin Hood, Prince of Thieves* used the beach, *Harry Potter and the Goblet of Fire* used a shot of the Seven Sisters cliff face, and the coastguard cottages and beach appeared in *Atonement*.

Although the path is extremely accessible as far as the beach, it suddenly stops and you will need to pull, push or carry anything with wheels. Walk on round to the east where the majestic white cliffs tower above. If it is picnic time, sit some distance from the cliffs, as chunks can fall off. Time to eat those 'Crumbling Cliff' buns you made earlier.

The sea has strong currents here, so close to the river mouth, and there are no lifeguards. However, children and beaches go together well, and here, with so many interesting pebbles, is the ideal opportunity for them to become sculptors. Suggest that they make a collection of flattish stones, then, using sand or tiny pebbles to secure them, build them up as high as you can. It can be quite tricky, but aesthetically pleasing, to create home-made 'Andy Goldsworthies'. Keen-eyed explorers can look out for fossils, too. Keep an eye on the tide.

To return, either retrace your steps, or walk west along the beach, and follow the river bank inland. There are also paths up on the hillside for the more energetic to enjoy.

GINA SAYS

"A really relaxing walk down to the beach alongside the river. Wear shoes that will be comfortable for hopping over rockpools and walking across pebbles. The Visitor Centre has some interesting info about the changing coastline, which I was surprised to find I knew a bit about already from geography at school!"

Getting there National grid ref. TV5197

❯ Buses: 12, 12A and 12B run frequently to Exceat from Brighton and Eastbourne.

❯ Useful website: www.sevensisters.org.uk, tel. 01323 870280.

THE CUCKOO TRAIL

ON YOUR BIKES!

R iding a bike is a very useful skill our children will probably value more and more as eco-friendly forms of transport become essential. I can remember stories told by grandparents who would think nothing of cycling 30 miles (48 km) to enjoy a picnic, or visit a sweetheart! While it is hard to imagine taking the family on such a jaunt on our very busy roads, thanks to the ever-increasing network of cycle paths it is possible to cycle safely for distances tailored to suit the biking skill and stamina of your party.

The Cuckoo Trail has many advantages for a family outing. It stretches between Heathfield and Polegate, with an extension to Hampden Park in Eastbourne, using part of the National Cycle Network (NCN) Route 21. This is part of the London to Paris Greenway, an Anglo-French project which aims to establish a mainly traffic-free route between the two capitals. So travelling along the Cuckoo Trail today might encourage our children to cycle from Polegate to Paris one day!

You can join the trail at various points along its length, and just do a short stretch, or the whole 11 miles (17.7 km), remembering that you have to pedal the same distance back. The trail runs on the path left behind when the tracks of the disused 'Cuckoo Line' railway were taken up. The nickname comes from the tradition of the first cuckoo of spring being heard on the April 14th each year at Heathfield Fair, where a cuckoo was released from a basket.

The line was opened in 1849, between Eastbourne and Eridge, carrying people and livestock, milk and animal feed. It was closed in stages between 1965 and 1968. The coming of the railway was life changing for the rural community. In Heathfield there were only two buildings in the High Street in 1875. Natural gas was discovered there around 1896, while drilling for water. No water was found, only 'a foul smell and rushing of wind'. A match was lit, and a 16-foot (5-metre) flame showed the presence of gas. The railway station was lit by gas for many years.

The trail is not completely removed from cars, as at various points along the route it crosses roads, often dipping quite steeply down to them. (The train would have crossed these on bridges.) There are barriers across the trail before you reach the roads, so it is essential to prime children to STOP and WAIT for you.

Large stretches of the route are level, with good surfaces, as it was built by the local councils in partnership with Sustrans, a charity which designs and builds routes for cyclists, walkers and people with disabilities. Although much of the trail passes through beautiful Sussex countryside, you will also find yourself doing short stretches on paths through modern housing estates.

On your marks...
Before the outing, have a good look at the family bikes. Are they the right size for your children? Rather like shoes, you suddenly realise they are too small, and a child has grown several centimetres since Christmas. Equip all the bikes with a basket or pannier, so one person doesn't become a resentful packhorse. Also, make sure brakes work; pump up the tyres; take lights and reflective strips or clothing, if you might be out after dark; pack a first aid kit; give everyone a bell; take a puncture repair kit; carry a gadget to measure how far you have pedalled; and last, but most important, wear helmets that fit well and fasten securely.

Get set...
Use sun cream and pack plenty of water. If the outing doesn't demand a full-scale picnic, take apples, cubes of cheese and flapjacks, packed

with apricots and raisins for energy. Write down a list of possible items for a 'scavenger hunt' along the way, and take a small bag for each child to store their treasures. Things they might collect include an acorn, an oak leaf, an unusual twig, a round pebble, something special (such as a beautifully marked feather). When my children were small we enjoyed singing this silly rhyme, with lots of emphasis on the last line. (They are now very embarrassed by it!)

> Here's Cyril on his cycle
> He cycles all the day,
> He likes to see the country
> Cycling all the way.
> So cycle, cycle Cyril,
> Show us what you do,
> Cycle, cycle Cyril
> Pooh! Pooh! Pooh!

Go!

Remind everyone about stopping and waiting for you, about ringing bells, giving way to other trail users, and generally 'looking after the countryside'. The route starts from the north in Heathfield and passes some houses and gardens. Soon the sound of birdsong takes over from the traffic hum. Keep an eye on those charging ahead as after half a mile there are two roads, one of which is very busy. Soon you are well on the way, with fields opening out and the first trailside picnic table coming in to view, with handy racks on which to lean your bike.

The way is level and tree-lined for summer shade. Carved sculptural benches are placed along the way. Can you spot the one which is a good 'IDEA'? First along the trail is Horam (toilet in car park). There are signposts showing directions and distances, of great interest to those who feel they have already done 'hundreds' of miles. Look out for the 'echo' tunnel, and stop for a good shout. You will know it by the unusual diagonal pattern of bricks overhead, and peeling mosaics. While cycling along the high embankments, it is rather awesome to think of the huge effort and skill that was involved building the railways.

Then comes Hellingly, 4½ miles (7 km) from Horam. It might be worth a brief detour to look at the rare, circular churchyard, built on a circular Saxon mound. This belongs to the Church of St Peter and St Paul, and is known as a 'Ciric'. (Gina has a mild fascination with churchyard inscriptions.) You will pass Hellingly Station, now a private house, an old water mill, and over the River Cuckmere. Look out for early purple orchids, butterflies and, of course, listen out for cuckoos. The mother lays her eggs in the nests of other birds. The young cuckoos push the other baby birds out of the nest, and secure all the food for themselves.

There are more urban hazards as you approach Hailsham, 1½ miles (2.5 km) from Hellingly; a traffic light crossing, a subway, and a road through a housing estate. Keep together and you'll be fine. There is a busy stretch of road south of Hailsham, the B2104, which has a pelican crossing for trail users. There are other small roads to cross, preceded by barriers, which provide for good practice of vital road safety skills.

Then on to Polegate, where you can, if you have the energy, continue on to Hampden Park, which has a splendid park and lake.

The Cuckoo Trail is great for a family outing as you can pick and choose where you start and finish, go from north to south or vice versa, The going is easy, and suitable for everyone from preschoolers with stabilisers to mountain-biking grandparents (we've seen lots of these). There are some inclines but nothing too daunting, and you can even pretend, if you are so inclined, that you are a train!

GINA SAYS

"I don't get many opportunities to ride my bike, as I live in town and can walk to school. So it's great to get a bit of speed up on a traffic-free trail, and have a laugh with my friends while my Mum coos at the flowers far behind us. The funniest thing was watching my brother swerve, hands in the air (showing off) to and fro across the path before being catapulted into some stinging nettles! He didn't find it so funny!"

Getting there   National grid refs. Polegate TQ582050/Heathfield TQ581215
❯ Train: Polegate and Heathfield both have railway stations.
❯ Bus: Polegate, Hellingly, Horam and Heathfield are all served by the 52 and 53.

DEVIL'S DYKE

GOOD FOR THE SOUL

One of the reasons we love going to Devil's Dyke is that, weather and season permitting, you can travel there on an open-top bus, leaving from near Brighton Pier, during the summer and at weekends. The bus journey is thrilling, a roller-coaster ride through narrow lanes, with the wind tangling your hair, great views and the sound of your children laughing as they bounce along! The beginning and end of the trip are fun too, looking down from the top deck on to the bustle of Brighton seafront.

The Dyke itself is good for walking and picnicking while watching daring hang-gliders launch themselves into nothingness from the steep north slopes of the Downs. The views on a clear day are exceptional. In fact no less a person than John Constable said that 'the view over the Weald was the grandest in the world'.

Why is it the Devil's Dyke?

There is a legend that the Devil was unhappy with the folk who lived behind the Downs, in the Weald. They were converting to Christianity and building churches in their villages. He decided to dig a way through the protective wall formed by the Downs, so the sea would rush through and drown them all. He began digging at Poynings, hurling the soil over his shoulders as he went. However, he disturbed an old lady, who lit a candle, which woke up her cockerel, who crowed loudly. Due to the light and the cock-a-doodle doing, the Devil thought that dawn was breaking. So he fled, leaving the steep, V-shaped ravine that we see today. The hills, formed where the lumps of earth fell to land, are now familiar landmarks such as Chanctonbury Ring (see p. 33). It makes a good story.

The Dyke Estate

It is extraordinary to think that at the end of the Victorian era there was a railway from Brighton especially to the Dyke, a funicular railway coming up the steep slope from Poynings, and a cable car stretching across the ravine. A Mr J. H. Hubbard bought the Dyke Estate in 1892, and made this former wilderness into an early 'theme park,' with a little railway running down the Dyke itself, a hotel, a billiard room, a camera obscura, a farm to supply the hotel, two bandstands and a fairground. As you walk about, look carefully into the grassy banks, and you might see hard bases, all that is left of Mr Hubbard's great enterprise.

On the grass to the north of the car park stands a large Art-Deco monumental seat, with an inscription saying that in 1925 the Duke and Duchess of York dedicated the Dyke Estate to the use of the public for ever. So it is now ours to enjoy (though managed by the National Trust). Close by are illustrations depicting the amazing views, labelling key features to be seen, for instance Toys Hill, the highest hill in Kent.

A good walk

By the bus stop is The Devil's Dyke Hotel (actually a pub-restaurant) and inside the doorway is a map showing three good walks, of varying length and difficulty. The green route is easy, the orange moderate, the purple hard. You know your troops! Signposts along the routes have helpfully coloured arrows to keep you on your intended path. At week-ends the National Trust has a trailer with information, and activity packs for children. Often young walkers seem to keep going if armed with a stick and an occasional chorus of 'The Grand Old Duke of York.' I'm also a believer in rationed treats: 'an apple when we reach that tree,' 'a biscuit when we're half way there' (this need not be accurate, the further the better) and perhaps an ice cream at the end, 'if you don't moan!'

To appreciate the full impact of the Dyke, the largest dry valley in the country, take the path starting behind the Devil's Dyke Hotel, which leads right down the 'spine' of the ravine, before climbing back up the northern slope, and finding a spot for a picnic. It is often breezy up on the Downs, so find a sheltered spot looking over the Weald, and sharp-eyed youngsters can spot the comings and goings of the villages and fields far below. Look out too for butterflies and flowers. It is said there are 50 sorts of plants in a square metre of downland turf.

After all that exercise and a hearty picnic, the return bus journey can be a welcome rest.

NETTLES & DOCKS

Make sure you can readily recognise a dock leaf in the field (botanical name *Rumex*). Nettle stings are almost an unavoidable hazard when out in the countryside, and dock leaves bring some relief, especially if you crunch them up a bit first, or split them to release the juice. Broad-leaved docks are the best, and are usually found wherever nettles grow. Some people rub the area with the leaf, others just place the leaf on top of the sting and press. Experiment for yourselves.

GINA SAYS

"I always love going on the open-top bus. The feeling of the wind whooshing round my face always seems to whip me up into excitement — it's very exhilarating! The Dyke is the perfect picnic spot and it's great to sit and eat while you watch the hangliders floating overhead, and wonder what you would do if they came crashing down on you."

Getting there   National grid ref. TQ258110

❯ Bus: 77 runs frequently from Brighton Pier daily during the summer. Weekends only out of season.

FRISTON FOREST

HUNTER GATHERING

We have enjoyed walking in Friston Forest, near Seaford for many years, long before we had children, and it was one of the places we couldn't wait to take them to after their arrival! With the baby strapped into a front pack we would march off at all times of the year, and at six months old Gina wouldn't be able to sleep that night, being so full of the images of downland and trees and big brother charging around showing her sticks and leaves. Later, and all a little older, we would climb up towards the Downs and have a picnic on a bench at the edge of the forest, looking north over the vast rolling fields. Then for a while it became part of the outing for my husband Mark and I to sit and be entertained by unrehearsed and improvised plays, put on with leaves and acorns as props. In fact, leaves would serve as tickets, programmes, costume accessories and even characters! Later still, we discovered the joys of food for free. So always have a clean plastic bag or two in your pocket, as you never know what bounty you might find to bring home.

I remember as a small child we always had an annual 'blackberry expedition', with Mum and Dad, big sister and her beau, Grandma and as many tin pails and bowls as we could fit in the car. It was autumn. My father's driving (he bought his licence, no test in those days) was always alarming and erratic, so we would arrive at the chosen hillside, wild place or his favourite 'Private Property', and all get out feeling a bit shaky. Then his battle with the methylated spirit cooker would commence, and a long time after that a strong cup of tea would set everyone up for a long stint in the blackberry bushes. Except of course Dad, who would settle down with his *News of the World* for a good sleep! Gradually one by one we dropped out – Grandma for a sit-down with a Butter Minto in the car, me to mess about whining, the beau to join Dad in a snooze – leaving Mum and sister urgently picking and chatting and planning. We would set off home with the car smelling fragrantly of leaves, berries and autumn, fingers stained and scratched, legs throbbing from the 'stingers'. And in the boot, buckets of glistening, juicy berries, adorned with tiny spiders trying to feel their way home.

HEDGEROW JAM

From *Jams, Pickles and Chutneys: the Best Kept Secrets of the Womens Institute* by Midge Thomas.

This is a recipe for jam that you can make when you get home with your haul. Of course, jam-making requires adult supervision, but smaller children can help with label making or making paper lids for the jam jars.

WHAT YOU NEED

- *8oz /225 g rose hips*
- *8oz /225 g haws*
- *8oz /225 g rowan berries*
- *8oz /225 g sloes*
- *1lb /450 g crab apples*
- *1lb /450 g blackberries*
- *1lb /450 g elderberries*
- *4oz /115 g chopped hazelnuts*
- *2lb /900 g sugar, plus the weight of the fruit pulp*

1. Wash and clean the fruit well. Put the rose hips, haws, rowan berries, sloes and crab apples in a large preserving pan and add water to cover. Cook for about an hour until all the fruit is tender.

2. Sieve the cooked fruits and weigh the resulting pulp. Put the pulp back into the washed preserving pan and add the blackberries, elderberries and chopped nuts. Simmer for about 15 minutes.

3. Add the 2lb/900 g of sugar plus as much extra sugar as the weight of the pulp. Cook over a low heat to dissolve the sugar then boil rapidly until setting point is reached. Remove any scum. Cool.

4. Pour into cooled, sterilised jars, seal and label.

Then came the great boiling, when the kitchen steamed and the sweet brambly scents attracted wasps and children, all keen to view the alchemy of turning fruit into jam. Of course I now realise that my mother planned ahead, collecting sufficient jars, stockpiling sugar and hoarding plenty of little plastic jam pot covers, although we always ran out and I had to dash off and buy more from the newsagent round the corner.

Although it is possible to make jam, or chutneys or pickles, from shop-bought ingredients, there is something deeply satisfying about surveying a line of freshly filled jars that have only cost the price of some sugar or vinegar. My children have caught the bug, and love to help, making labels and cutting circles of pretty fabric to adorn the lids.

Some tips for fruit picking: make sure you know what is edible; don't pick fruit lower down if it is accessible to dogs and other animals; don't pick at the sides of fields of cereals that have been sprayed (a growing crop usually indicates this); go a good distance from traffic before picking; a walking stick can be useful for hauling down higher branches; wear old gloves; wear stout shoes or wellies; don't mind if the younger pickers eat more than they collect, blackberries are good for you! Don't knock over the containers (this does happen).

Elderflowers are a really delicious ingredient. We love to make cordial, and always bring home a bag of creamy, fragrant flower heads when they come out at the end of May. If you don't have time to make cordial, push a flower head into a bottle of white wine or sparkling water. Chill for a few hours, and enjoy a refreshing drink on a warm evening.

Friston Forest

When you get to Friston Forest, you will find that there are two main car parks – one behind the Seven Sisters Country Park and another, slightly cheaper one, on Litlington Road, on the right-hand side travelling north. We tend to use this one as it is very spacious, with picnic tables around the edges, which on a pleasant day are very well used. There are many paths through the forest, with well-marked signs. One of these leads to the north, where you can view the chalk White Horse on the hillside across the valley.

Although there was a previous White Horse nearby, the one we look at today was made by three men – Mr Bovis, Mr Hobbis and Mr Ade – in 1924. Apparently they cut it one night by the light of a full moon, to surprise the local folk in the morning! It was camouflaged during the war so it couldn't be seen from the air by enemy aircraft and used as a landmark. Afterwards it had to be scoured back to its chalky whiteness. It is 90 feet (27.5 metres) high and a lovely sight across the valley.

The king & the cakes

Nestling in the forest north of the Exceat car park is the beautiful and very exclusive village of West Dean. It was probably a Saxon fishing and salt-producing village, sheltered in its valley. Alfred the Great had a palace in the village and we always wonder where it was. It is exciting to realise he was a real man who had a home in Sussex, not just a legend who burned cakes! He was born in AD 849 in Wantage, then in Berkshire, the youngest of five sons and one daughter. His father was named Aethelwulf, and his brothers were Aethelstan, Aethelbald, Aethelbert and Aethelred I. They all died defending their kingdom and so Alfred came to power in 871, aged only 22. He reigned for 28 years, dying in 899. Alfred spent part of his reign hiding from the Danes in the marshes of Athelney in Somerset. The legend of the cakes pertains to the time he was in hiding, sheltering in the home of a peasant woman who was making griddlecakes. He was supposed to keep an eye on them in case they burned, but didn't! Not knowing she was in the presence of a king, the woman told him off. Quite right too!

After building up his forces Alfred defeated the Danes. King Guthran agreed to become a Christian, and England was divided, the Danes having much of northern and eastern England, which became 'Danelaw'. Alfred was responsible for creating the first navy, and built many boats. There is some speculation that his naval base was at nearby Exceat, close to his palace at West Dean.

West Dean was badly affected by the Black Death, as was Exceat, which was abandoned in the 1450s. Wandering the peaceful pathways today it is fascinating to think of those Saxons who lived here. If your children have an interest in history, battles, ancient kingdoms and legends, this forest makes an ideal outing. Cardboard swords and crowns could be made at home beforehand, or improvise on the spot with sticks and leaves. Gina usually finds some lengths of grass to thread leaves and tie around her head.

Take a picnic, enjoy some stories of kings and queens, knights and battles and look out for some of the many creatures living in these beautiful beech woods. There are deer and badgers, barn owls (keep an eye out for the owl boxes on the trees on the White Horse trail) and butterflies in the sunny glades.

GINA SAYS

"Since I've been older we've carried on the walk a little bit further, up the slope and over the huge downland hills, then down one more grassy stretch to the village of Litlington. We are always starving by this time so are 'forced' to call in at the lovely Litlington Tea Gardens. The struggle back up the many hills on the way to the car park is always made easier after a hot jacket potato and a huge slice of cake!

It's also great because every time we come back from the woods laden with blackberries, I make a blackberry sponge cake which I absolutely adore (especially with a drop of cream)!"

Getting there   National grid ref. TQ518002

◗ Bus: 12, 12A and 12B run frequently to Exceat from Brighton and Eastbourne.

◗ Useful website: Friston Forest www.forestry.gov.uk

HASTINGS

FISH & MORE FISH

There is so much to see and do in Hastings. The town is vibrant, fun and 'real'– nowhere more so than at the far eastern end of the beach, where a fleet of working fishing boats makes a fascinating focal point for a visit. Most of us, especially children, are removed from the production and source of our food. However, we can learn about sustainable fishing from the brave folk who work here, and about the colourful history of the fishing industry in Hastings. A visit could inspire the making of model boats, and even a bit of amateur fishing too!

The Stade

This unusual and ancient word means, appropriately, landing place. Your visit could begin with a look in the lifeboat station. There, climb the steps beside a huge 'Talus' tractor, used to manoeuvre the lifeboat up and down the beach, and admire the smart navy and orange lifeboat, gleaming and ready to go to the rescue of anyone in trouble at sea. It looks so well maintained it could be brand new, so it is a bit of a shock to discover that *Sealink Endeavour* has already saved more than 40 lives. It is operated by volunteers, with only a coxswain and station mechanic being full-time staff. Sometimes you can see the crew training.

There is a display to show how boats look at night, with different lights sending different messages to the rescuers, for example, two red and two white lights, starboard view, mean 'vessel aground'. There are pieces of rope and directions to make a bowline knot strong enough to hold fast a boat when moored or being towed. My nimble-fingered daughter managed it straight away. I gave up!

Back outside, there is a pathway heading east, with 'walkways' leading down between weather-beaten sheds to the fishing boats. There are massive winches, used to haul the boats up the beach. Sniff the air and smell a heady mix of tar, ozone and, of course, fish. Listen to the sounds of seagulls, the flutter of flags on buoys and the constant swoosh of the waves on shingle. Rectangular cuttlefish pots are stacked neatly, and nets and ropes and cables are spread out over the beach, just as they must have been for hundreds of years, give or take some plastic!

The boats are short, stocky and sturdy looking, lined up along a high ridge of pebbles, valiantly facing the sea. On a bright, sunny day, with a pleasant breeze and gentle swell, the boats present a most cheerful picture. It is important to remember that often the sea is wild and rough, and the fishermen work in conditions we would find unacceptable and frightening, all to bring home fish for our tea.

One of our favourite songs, which seems appropriate to this visit even though it is originally from Northumberland, is *Dance to Your Daddy*.

> *Dance to your daddy, my bonnie laddie (lassie)*
> *Dance to your daddy, my bonnie lad.*
> *You shall have a fishie, on a little dishie,*
> *You shall have a fishie, when the boat comes in.*

There are lots of versions of the words, but this is the one we like best. Seeing a real fishing community brings home the courage and skill needed to provide that fishie!

On the Stade, towards the road and Rock-a-Nore station, are some strange, tall, narrow wooden buildings, painted black, called net shops. They are unique to Hastings and date back to Victorian times. They were used to store nets, which were made of natural material, and could rot. Nowadays, as seen on the beach, the nets are made of synthetic material and stored in huge plastic bags. The net shops, with their spooky 'Gormenghast' look, are more picturesque than the bags!

The Fishermen's Museum

Also on the Stade is the Hastings Fishermen's Museum, which is housed in the fishermen's church of St Nicholas, built in 1852. After World War II it fell into disuse. Fortunately, in 1956, some local people decided that the marvellous history of Hastings' fishing industry should be preserved, and used the church to house their collection of maritime artefacts. It took the demolition of part of a wall to push a splendid lugger into the building. As you will see, it is a snug fit to accommodate *The Enterprise*, one of the last sailing fishing boats.

The urge to climb on board will be strong and, happily, it is allowed. Imagine the waves rolling beneath you, salty smells and creaking timbers. Then notice there is nothing to hold on to! The sides of the boat were made deliberately low, as hauling the nets up and over would have required great strength. A helpful gentleman at the museum explained that a knee would be used to hold on to the net, as the next section was hauled up.

As you climb back down, notice the lugger is almost flat bottomed, shaped to be pushed and pulled over the beach. Before the days of the powerful electric winches, horses were used to drag the boats up, by rising Horse Capstans, and there is an example of one here with pictures showing the horses at work. As a boat approached the beach, a hawser attached to a capstan was hooked onto its stern. A horse harnessed to the capstan's long bar pulled the boat beyond the high-water mark.

The horses belonged to the council and were also used for collecting refuse. In the 1930s the council replaced the horses with lorries, and quite amazingly, seemed to hope that the fishing industry would move along the coast to Rye. Fortunately winches could do the job of the horses, so the fishermen stayed put. Throughout the history of Hastings, it appears the fishermen have had a hard a struggle to stay on the Stade. Even as recently as the 1950s, the council planned to clear the beach for redevelopment. Nowadays, the Hastings fishermen are committed to sustainable fishing and are receiving well-deserved praise and recognition for their environmentally friendly methods.

Climb back down, and begin again, looking at the numerous fascinating sea-related displays. It is a museum to move around slowly, as it is so packed with objects, paintings and photos. Old paintings showing the boats lined up on the beach could be mistaken for the present day, except for the sails.

There are nets, anchors, huge hooks, models of luggers and a stuffed Great Wandering Albatross, shot in the Atlantic in 1890. Look out for the two swordfish blades with sharp saw edges, and shudder. Don't miss the extraordinary suit, at first glance resembling 'Pearly King' attire, and realise it is covered in winkle shells, painted silver, made and worn by Walter 'Slogger' Hoad. In fact, many of the fishermen mentioned in the museum have nicknames. The Winkle Club is a benevolent institution set up to help underprivileged families of the Old Town.

Biddy the Tubman, a local character, who as a lifeboat man saved 46 lives, used to entertain holidaymakers by paddling along in an old fish tub, and there are some very funny photos of him. At the back of the museum you can watch a most dramatic film, showing the landing of a fishing boat on the Stade in extremely wild conditions. We were completely gripped, and the episode conveys clearly what a risky job fishing is.

Outside the museum, there are more fine boats to admire, plus 'Half Sovereign Cottage,' made from half a boat. Boats were often built with false bottoms to conceal smuggled goods. When these were discovered, the boats were 'torn asunder at midships'. Some of the resulting half boats became little shacks. Along the road, shops and stalls sell locally caught fish, in case you haven't been tempted to catch your own!

GINA SAYS

"Oh how I'd love to be a member of the Winkle Club! Not sure what would be involved but I love the name! And the outfit! Apparently royal visitors to Hastings and the Winkle Club receive golden winkle brooches, which sound pretty.

Also the Sovereign Cottage is so lovely. A bit small to live in perhaps but I think several in a row making up one home would be perfect for me and maybe the dog. The little rowing boats are great too, so Captain Jack!"

Getting there   National grid ref. TQ826094
❯ Train: services from London, Brighton and Ashford.
❯ Car: Hastings is on the A259, A21 and A2101.

HIGHDOWN HILL

BLOWIN' IN THE WIND

We think Highdown Hill, just outside Worthing, is a great place for breathing in some fresh air while charging to and fro trying to get your kite airborne! There are few trees or other overhead obstacles that can ruin the day, just plenty of windy space, with wonderful views of the sea and the Weald.

Recycled kites

You might feel like making your own kite, and if so you can be as sophisticated, simple, decorative or plain as you please. A quick glance at the internet will furnish you with many patterns and diagrams to follow. Some folk make effective kites from big bin bags. We prefer a more traditional diamond shape, made from brightly coloured or printed plastic bags. We have tried several, and I have to admit that the fun has been more in the construction than in the flying but you may have more aeronautical skills than we do!

Whether home-made, borrowed or bought, there is something very pleasing and exhilarating about the feeling of the wind tugging at the kite high above your head. Small children will need help, although try not to let them see you are doing it. In any case, you usually need one person to hold on tight, while the other stands some distance away, to do the launching. If, after those efforts, things literally come down to earth with a bump, be distracted by a bracing walk around the hill.

KITE INSTRUCTIONS

Fig. 1

Fig. 2

Fig. 3

Fig. 4

Fig. 5

Fig. 6

YOU WILL NEED

- *Sheet of paper 8¹/₂ in (22 cm) x 11 in (28 cm)*
- *Bamboo barbeque skewer 8¹/₂ in (22 cm) long*
- *Material for 'tail', such as 10-in (25-mm) wide plastic tape or plastic bag cut into long thin strip, approx 6 feet (2 metres) long*
- *Roll of ¹/₂-in (15-mm) wide sticky tape*
- *Roll of string (allow about 10-13 feet (3-4 metres) per kite)*
- *Piece of cardboard for winding the string round*

1. Fold paper in half.

2. Fold diagonally along line AB.

3. Fold back one side and tape along fold line AB.

4. Place bamboo skewer along line CD and tape down firmly.

5. Tape 'tail' to point B.

6. Turn kite over and pull centre flap away from the sides so it stands proud. Punch hole in flap at point E and tie roll of string here, then wind remaining string around a folded piece of card.

Near to the car park and picnic tables, there stands a tomb, with iron railings round. It belonged to John Olliver, an eccentric miller, who had a reputation for being a rogue and a joker. Some 27 years before his death, in 1793, he had the tomb erected on the hill, then built a small wooden shack at the head of the tomb, where he spent many happy hours! It was said he was a smuggler and used the tomb to store his contraband. Apparently he set his mill sails to act as signals to the smugglers out at sea. When he eventually died, aged 84, over 2,000 members of the public came to his funeral, and rioting ensued. Eight ladies dressed in white drew his coffin, and it is said that he had arranged to be buied vertically, upside down!

The hill was occupied through the Bronze Age, Iron Age, Roman and Anglo-Saxon times. There are ramparts and ditches, and evidence of a Saxon cemetery, which was exposed during the great storm of 1987, when so many trees were uprooted. And on Midsummer Night you will hear the bells of the Morris Men who come to make merry on this ancient site.

The Chalk Garden

If you would like a more sheltered spot for a picnic, the Highdown Chalk Garden is the perfect place. The creation of this lush, verdant garden began in 1909, by a far-sighted gentleman, Sir Frederick Stern, in an old chalkpit. We have enjoyed visiting here with our children for many years, and we always find something new to see. Little pathways curve this way and that, opening out into areas of beautifully mown grass, beds of exotic agapanthus, lilies so tall and pink they look like flamingos, and a fine pond. This is home to several huge fish, almost 2 feet (60 cm) long, gold and black, who spend the day gently nudging the surface and slipping back under the many lily pads.

Because the garden is laid out in a series of 'rooms', sheltered by the high chalk cliff, there is much to see. While there is always a quorum of keen plantsmen, admiring the inspiring combinations of blooms, and the skill of Stern's gardeners in persuading so much to grow in chalk, there is usually the sound of happy children, too.

We love to look at the dedications on plaques and benches, and imagine the people who inspired them. Can you find one dedicated to an extremely happy person? His inscription read s: 'Laugh and the world laughs with you' and 'Always look on the bright side of life'. We like to make them up – 'Could always spot a bargain', 'Never silent till now', 'Don't sit here, it's my bench' and so on. The suggestions inevitably become too rude, or silly, and we have to stop.

The Highdown goblet

If the weather turns nasty, there is a fine museum in the heart of Worthing (the Worthing Museum and Art Gallery) which is always great to visit with children as it really does have something to interest everyone. Nowadays Gina is always drawn to the costume galleries, spanning three centuries of fashion; when she was younger it was the Victorian toy collection she loved.

After a visit to Highdown Hill it is particularly interesting to look at the 'Highdown Goblet', in the archaeology gallery. This Ancient Egyptian glass vase with an Ancient Greek inscription was found in the Anglo-Saxon cemetery at Highdown. It is amazing to think that this beautiful green glass goblet, decorated with a dog chasing a hare and an inscription 'Drink me and good health to you', has survived intact for so long.

GINA SAYS
"The grass is brilliant for cartwheels. Also a great place for hide-and-seek.

It's a lot of fun finding hidden pathways to wander along, or be chased down by a brother. Even falling over on that grass doesn't hurt – it's really soft. Perfect for toddlers.

Also, look out for the sundial in the Millennium Garden. It really does tell the time on a sunny day, if you remember to add an hour in the summer."

Getting there   National Grid ref TQ095042
❷ Car: west of Worthing on the A259.
❷ Useful website: Highdown Chalk Gardens www.highdowngardens.co.uk, tel, 01803 501054.

HORSHAM PARK & MUSEUM

A DAY ON THE TOWN

Sometimes it isn't appropriate to head off into the 'wilds' for a day out. A well-planned park with well-planned play equipment and accessible facilities, close to shops, services and good transport links, can do very nicely. Horsham Park is fortunate to have these features, and more. We feel it can be a lovely outing for everyone, from toddlers to grandparents, and the attractive pedestrian shopping streets of the town are only five minutes away, so restless teenagers can lope off to window-shop.

Preplanning can make the outing even better. Arriving at an expanse of lovely grass without a ball or frisbee can result in recriminations and sulking. Coffee, juice and sandwiches times four or five can cost a great deal, whereas if you take your own, you can appear to be very generous with ice creams and treats! I find it helpful to pack one container with a large cut-and-come-again type of cake. We have differently coloured plastic beakers for each person's water, so there are no accusations of 'that's my cup, I don't want your germs !' Some children happily swig from a communal water bottle, wiping the top with a grubby fist before passing it on, but that can be avoided.

Instead of a picnic blanket for the children we sometimes take the mat (and arrows) from a game of Twister. Dual function: sit on and play on! At Horsham Park there is a large sand play area, so pack buckets and spades. There is also a skate park for keen skateboarders.

The park is right by a leisure centre, 'The Pavilions in the Park,' which is well signposted. The adventure playground is alongside the Pavilions. It covers a large area with equipment suitable for children up to the age of 14. There is a zip-wire, climbing net, assault course, and many dangling, revolving, wobbly things to test balance and patience. The brightly coloured equipment seems in good repair and sits in pleasantly landscaped surroundings.

The climbing frame for younger children looks fun too, as does the big sand area and jolly sit-on animals. There are picnic tables, and even a drinking fountain, in a garden area, with information about saving water. The whole playground is safely fenced and gated, so dogs can't come in, and roving toddlers can't slip out easily. My son, when he was aged two, was always ready to make his escape, so I could never relax!

Close by the play area is the Millennium Maze, a charming waist-high affair, just taller than the heads of the preschoolers bumbling around it, but convenient for the adults who can watch and direct from above. In the centre is a lovely dragon sculpture by Hannah Holmes, depicting the dragon of nearby St Leonard's Forest (*see p. 80*), referred to in legends of the area. The Park House Garden is a delightful sensory garden, accessible to the disabled and visually impaired. There are large grassy areas for ball games, races and tag, a permanent orienteering course for the very energetic, the skate park and a lake. There is a café near the maze, and another close by the leisure centre.

Horsham Museum

If the weather becomes inclement, or a change of focus is required, the splendid and fascinating Horsham Museum is only ten minutes walk away from the park. Follow signs through the park to the town centre. There is a bright underpass, with a cheerful mosaic depicting all kinds of food, leading to Carfax, past a castellated town hall, and into Causeway. The museum is housed in a medieval timber-framed building at number 9 Causeway. There has been a building on the site for 900 years. The present timber-framed rooms forming part of the building date back to the 1420s and 30s.

THE BRILLIANT BOOTH

If you enjoy the eccentricities of Horsham Museum, you might also like the Booth Museum in Hove. Mr Edward Booth, a Victorian ornithologist, created his collection of stuffed birds in 1874. Here, numerous cases of birds display the taxidermist's art, showing their beautiful plumage in their natural habitats. There are fossils, rocks and minerals, insects in amber and beautiful butterflies, so lovely and so sad, pinned into their display cases. And best of all for many young naturalists is the large collection of skeletons, from a tiny pygmy shrew to a whale.

This would be a rewarding outing for grandparents and older friends to accompany children on, as there is so much that would remind them of their own childhood and precipitate discussions between the generations. The museum is very atmospheric, the displays leading one to another in a series of recreated shops, workshops and cabinets. There is a chemist's shop with mysterious potions and powders, a blacksmith's, an equestrian shop, a wheelwright's workshop and a gruesome display of prison artefacts. Look into a prison cell at a poor soul languishing on his bed. Gasp at the horrifying neck chains and leg irons, huge keys and a vast lock. You can press a switch to 'look at the face of a killer, through the spy hole in the door'. We didn't dare!

Upstairs there is such a variety of displays, including a Once Upon a Time Room, packed with toys, dolls' houses, children's clothes and wonderful Mabel Lucy Atwell china. Turn a wheel and the display goes round. Press a switch and the dolls' house lights up and the little model train goes to and fro. There are toys and books to interest all ages.

In another gallery is a charming display of shells, right beside a fearsome collection of African weapons including lethal looking Masai spears. The Cabinet of Curiosities shows how wealthy people in the 16th century would display their collections of man-made and natural objects, from all over the world. How amazing these exotic things would seem to folks who never left Horsham. Of great interest too are the dinosaur bones and fossils found locally, of a *Polacanthus rudgewickensis*, named after the nearby Rudgewick Brickworks where it was discovered. Three iguanodons have also been found at Horsham.

The museum even has a delightful garden to explore, with a barn exhibiting farming-related artefacts, and another with a collection of carts, including one to be pulled by a goat or dog! Gina rather hoped we might get one, to go with her ambition to own a goat!

The museum has so much to see, we always hope to return again soon.

GINA SAYS

"I love the little museum, it's so atmospheric. Then of course my heart went out to those beautiful riding boots. I can't bear that they're so old and they may never be worn again, poor things! However, I cheered up at the sight of 65 pairs of shoes displayed in drawers you could pull out to get a closer look. Mum went a bit teary eyed though because so much of what was displayed (Oxo boxes — whatever they were! Biscuit tins and ancient Coca-Cola adverts) could have been straight out of her childhood. The whole place is just really lovely.

While we are talking about museums, I'd like to mention the Booth Museum; It's really cool to see so many butterflies close up, as you would never normally see them. They have kind of furry bodies which are an interesting contrast to their fragile, delicate wings. And the bears at the entrance always make you jump!"

Getting there   National grid ref. TQ170304

◉ Train: there is a mainline railway station.
◉ Bus: good bus services from surrounding areas.
◉ Useful websites: Horsham Park www.horshampark.org; Horsham Museum
   www.horshammuseum.org; Booth Museum www.booth.virtualmuseum.info

HEAVENLY HOVE

MUSEUMS & BEACHCOMBING

A great day out can be enjoyed in Hove and, as it is very flat, it is ideal for cycling too. Our trip combines culture and nature, and starts at the magical Hove Museum, in New Church Road. It then heads down the road to the sea and west along to the Hove Lagoon playground. Try to plan the seashore part of the day to coincide with low tide, and preferably a calm sea.

Hove Museum

Hove Museum is housed in an Italianate Victorian villa. It has been refurbished and is accessible to all, with a great café and lovely little shop, which often sells work by featured artists. Outside the museum is a very distinctive structure, the Jaipur Gate. It was made for an exhibition opened by Queen Victoria in Kensington, London, in 1886, and formed part of the entrance to exhibition courts showing Indian art. The gate was designed by two Englishmen and carved by Indian craftsmen. The motto of the Maharajas of Jaipur is carved in English, Sanskrit and Latin 'Where virtue is, there is victory'. A Latin inscription on the back reads: 'From the east comes light', which, of course, is true.

The downstairs galleries hold changing exhibitions. My children still remember one year when there were great 'pods' to climb inside, which they desperately wanted as bedrooms! The café walls display paintings, and cabinets hold collections of beautiful jugs, plates and Toby jugs.

Upstairs, find the gallery of Modern Artefacts. There are three themes; Alchemy, Inspiration and Making. The process of working in different materials is explored and the artists describe their inspiration. Look out for *Pleated Vessel Form 1998* by James Cox, in resin, copper and fabric, which manages to be both abstract and look like a bending torso at the same time.

A panel on the wall says inspiration is anything that motivates creativity. It mentions the relevance of keeping a notebook, and that is indeed how many artists record and remember things that inspire them. I love the fact that jeweller Cynthia Cousins has used the inspiration of the winter landscape of the Downs in making her beautiful silver necklaces. She says drawing is the key to her work. Many types of materials are used to create these modern pieces, for instance the 'winged insect' made from grass, and the wool and grass 'flower'.

Leaving that gallery, look down into the illuminated circle in the floor, at a magical halo-like creation, made with nylon filament. It reminds me of creatures of the deep, in either sea or space! Spot the little insects hiding in the leaves of the ironwork railings. Here more artists describe their inspiration: travelling, weather, even everyday routines. Look out for a cabinet of stiletto shoes made from paper, and a cup and saucer by Lucy Rie (my favourite potter), hand thrown but so fine, the dark rim emphasising the form.

In the local history room you can see the skull of an Anglo-Saxon woman, of the seventh or eighth century, and Gina noted how perfect her remaining teeth were! Also, an enormous tooth from an elephant, found here in Hove, dating from when Great Britain was joined to Europe. The room full of paintings changes its display from time to time.

Then to the Wizard's Attic, which is a joy. The wizard snoozes above your head in a hammock, suddenly doing a loud snore. Watch people jump! This room really is a 'box of delights'. It combines things in strange ways, rather like a dream. A cabinet shaped like an old-fashioned hooped skirt is filled with Action Man figures. Pop your head (if you are small) up into the middle of a group of toy farm animals. Peer into the toy mender's shop, there is a 'mouse hole' to creep into and toy soldiers march inside a tin bath. Look at the dolls' houses and a vintage pedal car flying overhead. Then there are the cabinets of dolls, creepy and fascinating at the same time. Drawers open, with more dolls and, gruesomely, parts of dolls, made from different materials, all to feel! Not for the squeamish. There are trains, cars and a child's bedroom filled with a clever mixture of old and modern toys. It is important to give yourselves plenty of time in these galleries, as there is so much to see.

Going beachcombing
I find that a visit to somewhere like Hove Museum can act as a catalyst, prompting the urge to 'make things'. As so many children spend hours cocooned with a television or computer, the impulse to make and do needs rekindling. The beach, any beach, can be a great resource. I know artists who make a living turning flotsam and jetsam into works of art. Flotsam originally meant cargo or wreckage floating on the sea, while jetsam is cargo or waste thrown overboard, then eventually washed up on the beach. The two words now imply anything on the beach that you wouldn't expect to find there.

So become beachcombers for the day, remembering bags to carry home your treasures. The term beachcomber first appeared in print in 1847, describing a group of Europeans living in the South Pacific Islands, who 'combed' the beaches for flotsam and jetsam. Nowadays, we use the term to describe that dreamy, timeless activity of drifting along, gazing closely at the beach beneath your feet, collecting what you can.

The seafront is a short walk from the museum, heading south. At the beach, turn west towards the Lagoon. Follow some safety rules: tell everyone not to pick up anything that looks dirty, oily or sharp and to show a grown-up anything they are not sure about before collecting; keep an eye on the sea, an incoming tide can catch you by surprise with a sudden big wave.

If the sea has been rough in the preceding days, larger objects will have been thrown up. A retreating tide will leave behind a trail of interesting bits and pieces to retrieve. Look out for shells, 'mermaid's purses' (dogfish egg-cases), cuttlefish bones, lengths of brightly coloured plastic rope, corks, fishing floats and pieces of driftwood. Smoothed by the sea, these can be the basis of an imaginative creation, perhaps painted and tied around with some bright plastic string. Your finds can also trigger some impromptu storytelling. We recently found a single diving flipper and wondered what had happened to the diver.

Back home, rinse your finds in clean water, taking care not to chip fragile shells, and leave to dry. Small children will enjoy painting and gluing everything, then sprinkling with glitter. More skilful artists can let their imaginations run free, making collages, sculptures and even mobiles to hang from coat hangers. Remember, these creations will look really great in your children's bedrooms, not necessarily in the living room!

Nearly at the end of the beach is an excellent playground, with a paddling pool for the very young and exciting equipment to climb and swing on. My children have always loved it here by the sea. There is a café too, and a skateboard and BMX park. You can even watch learner windsurfers and sailors practising on the Lagoon, and be further inspired to learn a new skill.

This outing can easily be adapted to Worthing, where there is a most inspiring museum (see p. 59), which again is very child friendly. There are huge beaches and the wonderful Brooklands Park, opposite the seafront to the east of the town.

GINA SAYS

"My favourite things in the whole museum have to be the Dangerous Dolls, by Judy Dwyer. They're rather unconventional, decorative dolls made of painted silk, recycled tin, wire and resistors. Every one is unique and has its own personality or character, like boy or girl, human or animal (they often seem to be a mix of the two!) and good or evil. I think they are beautiful in a way, but they also have a slightly dark, even creepy look about them!

Also keep your wits about you in the kids' section! It's SO scary!"

Getting there   National grid refs. Hove Museum TQ280050 / Hove Lagoon TQ270046

● Bus: frequent service from Churchill Square in Brighton to Hove Museum and along the seafront to Hove Lagoon.

● Train: Hove railway station is within easy walking distance.

PETT LEVEL

FOR EXPLORERS

Most of the young children I know love being explorers. With a pair of binoculars (with safety fastening for quick release) around their necks and a magnifying glass in hand, they can spend hours investigating the world. You can extend this activity by equipping them with a few 'bug boxes' and an insect, plant or marine life identification book. However, at Pett Level you can become explorers searching for those most thrilling of finds, dinosaur footprints and fossils!

Pett Level beach is a bit of a surprise. There is a high sea defence wall running along the side of the long, straight road, obscuring views of the sea. You might not think to stop, but if you do, walk up the ramp beside the Smugglers pub and an interesting sight will greet you. If the tide is out, that is. For down on the exposed sand, what appear to be rather seaweedy rocks are actually the remains of a forest! Like many beaches Pett Level is best appreciated when the tide is going out. There are large boulders in places, and very young children will definitely need a hand. The sea leaves wonderful rockpools, and there are patches of sand, too, for some good digging. As on any expedition, remember to take a back-pack for bringing home 'specimens', while leaving your hands free.

Walk along to the west, past two interesting castellated houses, and cliffs begin to rise up. Cliff End is where the Wealden sandstone cliffs reach their easternmost point. It is *very important* to keep right away from the base of the cliffs here. Further round the headland is Fairlight Cove, where due to coastal erosion cliffs are collapsing, and several homes have already fallen over the receding edge. A wave barrier was completed in the 1990s but this only protects a limited area. Also, don't hammer near the cliffs; the vibration could result in a large collapse.

The cliffs and foreshore are comprised of layers of sandstone and clay, deposited approximately 140 million years ago by freshwater rivers. This area was part of the European landmass and was much nearer to the equator, and so had a subtropical climate, with conifer-type trees and ferns. As you walk and scramble along the beach, notice the layers in the cliffs, very different to the chalk cliffs in other parts of Sussex and Kent.

The petrified forest further down the beach, seen sticking out of the mud at low tide, probably belonged to the now extinct family of ferns, the *Tempskyacea*. The forest is thought to be 5,000 years old, and it is interesting to look at the trunks, roots and branches and imagine the sea level gradually rising as ice melted, drowning the forest. The wood is preserved in mud, which the tide is wearing away, exposing it to view. The sand here has a reddish tinge, and on the foreshore as the tide goes out, you will find many beautiful shells.

On the exposed foreshore there are footprints belonging to both carnivorous and herbivorous dinosaurs. The iguanodon tracks at Fairlight Cove are huge: they are three toed, with grooves behind them, which may have been made by their tails. As you explore the rocks, you become convinced that everything is a dinosaur footprint! One lady we spoke to said she had been sitting peacefully on a rock gazing at the view when a geologist strode up to her and said, 'Madam, you are sitting on a dinosaur footprint!' Do take a camera, as children especially will enjoy comparing their own footprints with those of an iguanodon and having photographic evidence of their discoveries.

Also on the foreshore, if you are lucky, you may find many different types of fossil, and occasionally dinosaur, crocodile and turtle bones, which tend to be dark brown in colour and have a pitted surface. More common are the fossils of the bivalve *Neomiodon*, on the surface of boulders on Pett beach. They look like present-day shells, but these are apparently freshwater creatures.

Stroll along slowly, looking carefully as you go, and who knows what prehistoric freshwater shark's tooth or fish skeleton you might find. Just look out for the incoming tide, which could catch you unawares, as fossil hunting, like rockpooling, is a very absorbing activity.

On the clifftops above this extraordinary beach is Hastings Country Park Nature Reserve. So when the tide comes in you can continue exploring there, as there are so many interesting birds, insects and plants to find. Within the Firehills area, nearest to Pett Level, are two 'access for all trails', starting at the car park and visitor centre, which have wonderful views and picnic areas. You can, on a clear day, see beyond Dungeness to the white cliffs of Dover. The park is a Site of Special Scientific Interest and a Special Area of Conservation, so you can be sure of finding something to 'explore'.

Grey Owl

In the car park is a memorial to Grey Owl, a Hastings man whose real name was Archie Belaney. He lived a life of extraordinary deception, pretending to be a Native American Indian. He was raised in Hastings by his grandmother and two stern maiden aunts, and loved roaming the hills above the town, developing his life-long interest in natural history. North American history and culture obsessed him, and when he was 18 he went to Canada, where he became a trapper and learned the Ojibway language. He then reinvented himself as the son of an Apache mother and Scottish father and claimed to be an adopted member of the Ojibway Tribe. He dyed his hair black, learned to canoe and survive in the wilderness.

During his 'marriage' to an Iroquois woman, Anahareo, he abandoned trapping, and began to write articles and books about the damage being done to the wilderness and the old ways of life. His fame spread and he became a celebrity. His books became bestsellers, and he made two lecture tours to Britain, even coming back to Hastings, in his full Native American costume, where his aunts, sitting in the audience, recognised him! He performed to the Royal Family, including the Princesses Margaret and Elizabeth, who were very enthusiastic about his thrilling storytelling. Although many people must have guessed the true identity of Grey Owl, no one exposed him publicly, not even his five 'wives'! The facts came out after he died in 1938, aged 50, but the truth of his message of conservation was seen as valid and genuine.

Grey Owl was fascinated by beavers and studied them at close quarters. While there are no beavers in Hastings Country Park, there are many rare insects, including the only tarantula-like spider in Britain, the purse-web spider, and a large population of dormice. Many birds stop off at the park when migrating, and the cliffs provide nesting sites for sea birds and peregrine falcons. Binoculars would be very handy for birdwatching here, and from the clifftops bottlenose dolphin and harbour porpoise can occasionally be seen. Grey Owl would approve.

To the south of the car park are networks of little paths between the gorse bushes – ideal for exploring and games of hide and seek – and lots of benches, perfect for picnicking when the ground is damp. If your party is feeling very energetic, paths lead westwards through beautiful Fairlight and Ecclesbourne Glens and then all the way to Hastings, where in the Hastings Museum and Art Gallery there is a reconstruction of Grey Owl's cabin.

GINA SAYS

"Whenever we go to Pett Level, I take my chance to build up my shell collection, while the boys hunt for fossils.

It's amazing because every single little shell is unique. They come in all differ-ent colours and with different patterns and markings on them – they can be extremely decorative, though they look best mixed together by the sea!

I always seem to find teeny-weeny shells – white, mussel-shaped ones that look like fairy wings nestling in the sand. I also love finding shells where the two halves are still attached to each other, so you can open and close them. Be careful when leaping across the big rocks though – some wobble! If you see any furry green stuff on the rocks, beware of that too because it is very, very, very slippery!"

Getting there   National grid ref. TQ887133
- Bus: 344 runs between Hastings and Rye, stopping at Pett Level.
- Useful website: Hastings Country Park Nature Reserve www.wildhastings.org, tel. 01424 813225.

PETWORTH PARK

PICNICS & PAINTINGS

T his beautiful parkland appears to be a natural landscape, combining trees, hills and lakes in a way that pleases the eye and invites exploration. It is surprising, therefore, to learn that it is man-made! We have become used to 'garden makeover' programmes on television, usually involving urban gardens and a trip to the garden centre and builders merchant. How amazing then, to look out at the rolling parkland of Petworth, and realise the vista you see is created by man. One man, in fact, the impressively named Lancelot 'Capability' Brown, without whose skills no 18th-century landowner could do.

Capability Brown (1716-83) worked for the third Earl of Egremont from 1753 to 1765. He was expert in making the contrived appear natural on a vast scale, and the rich and fashionable aristocracy were keen to secure his services. He therefore designed over 170 parks, and Petworth is considered to be his masterpiece. He apparently refused to work in Ireland, as he 'had not finished England'!

He was a master of damming, and created Petworth's serpentine lake, 'Upper Pond', using vast quantities of soil and clay. Some of the trees gracing the park date from his time, and continued planting of his favoured trees means future generations will be able to enjoy the parkland as he intended. All this means that Petworth Park makes a very congenial destination for a good walk and a picnic, as the vistas you enjoy have been artfully contrived to give pleasure to the beholder.

Grow a tree!

If visiting the park, or other deciduous woodland, in the autumn (or late summer, as the seasons seem to be moving ever forward) take the opportunity to encourage the 'Capability' in your children. You will need some used envelopes, a tree identification book and a pen to note the finder's name and the species of tree on the envelopes.

The aim is to collect a good selection of conkers, sycamore wings and acorns, striving to find ones that are as perfect as possible. Wormholes and mouldy bits won't do. Take them home and plant in pots, using compost or even garden soil. Water occasionally, talk to them (children, among others, are not embarrassed to do this) and hopefully they will germinate ready for planting in the spring. The little trees could make Christmas or birthday presents, with the pots gift-wrapped in recycled wrapping paper or even newspaper, and a label, or lolly stick, describing the species, provenance and name of the gardener!

Of course this will lead on to exciting games of conkers, so bring some lengths of string and something sharp to pierce holes. I find very young children are always delighted by sycamore key helicopters, which if launched from a high point (standing on a log) or by a tall person, twirl and spin round, excellent for practising catch. Simple activities such as these, which elicit giggles and shrieks of delight, are life-enhancing for everyone concerned, and we should do them more often.

Petworth Park is large, 750 acres (304 hectares), and it is a long walk from the North Car Park to the house and Upper Pond. This is the car park we use when we want to 'make a day of it'. Although there are various pedestrian access points, if carrying a picnic and accompanying paraphernalia, perhaps this car park is not the most convenient for toddlers and other folk who may not wish to do a long hike.

A sign in the car park points left for 'Pedestrians', but this is really just to show the way on foot to Petworth House. Straight ahead takes you through trees to a 200-foot (60-metre) climb up Monument Hill, where there are spectacular views of the South Downs, Blackdown and the Dorking Hills. From there follow the path down to Snow Hill, and enjoy the views across Upper Pond to Petworth House.

WATERCOLOUR TIPS

If your children have been suitably inspired by the fabulous views of the park and house by that master of the watery splodge, J.M.W. Turner, then why not set them up in a quiet corner of the park and let them release their own inner artist? Now, anyone who has ever tried to paint with watercolour knows how quickly it can all turn into a muddy mess. It would be a shame if your budding future Turner Prize winners were put off by the challenges of layered washes or the wet-in-wet technique at their first attempt. So leave the paints at home and take instead watercolour pencils and sticks. These are used just like a traditional pencil or crayon but when water is applied on top with a brush, their marks magically start to behave like paint. Great fun and much easier to control than pans or tubes of paint.

Turn left from the car park and head roughly south. Most paths lead past Lower Pond and then on towards Upper Pond, alive with honking geese and darting dragonflies. Petworth House seen from the lake impresses with its size and symmetry, and instead of formally laid out gardens, the parkland rolls right up to the house walls. This means you can run right up to the house, and even peer in the windows at some of the treasures within.

One of Petworth's most distinguished visitors was artist and painter, Joseph Mallord William Turner (1775-1851), and a guest of the third Earl. Turner painted the house, lake and grounds. He was a master of landscape painting, and became known as 'the painter of light'. It is said that his dying words were 'the sun is God'.

The deer

When we last visited Petworth it was autumn, and I think we must have seen every one of the herd of 1,000 fallow deer which live in the park! As we walked from car park to house, their heads popped up to watch us. Then, following some unseen signal, away they went, streaming across the path ahead of us, it was magnificent. One lady said it was just like being in the Serengeti, although I can't confirm that!

By the Upper Pond is a stone boathouse with stone seats, perfect for sitting and sketching the ducks and swans, or picnicking if the grass is too damp. Walk on along the path, round a grassy hillock (no doubt contrived by Mr 'C.' Brown) and there is the house. As you walk towards it, get the children to count the windows. Behind you, in the lake, is a statue of a dog, sculpted by John Carew, erected by the third Earl as a memorial to his favourite hound, which had drowned there. You could eat your picnic in front of the house and pretend for a while to be Lord Egremont, or Turner, sitting under the gaze of the noble busts above the windows.

Walking back towards the car park, the path leads through woods where you will find a wonderful tree trunk, some 9 feet (2.7 metres) in diameter, lying on its side just waiting to be turned into a pirate ship. There are oak, sweet chestnut and beech trees, with leaves and seeds to collect, and sticks to float on the Lower Pond as you pass by, admiring the natural yet contrived landscape of Capability Brown. His ideas went out of fashion, being criticised for not being as good as the real thing, but his Petworth Park still lends itself to a lovely day out.

GINA SAYS

"I'm a big fan of all things Jane Austen, and I can so imagine any one of her many heroines flitting about Petworth, bonnet and all!

However, I've got a bit of a dilemma. I think maybe I would have to extend our back garden a bit to fit the deer in. I think they're just so beautiful. Such big brown eyes and deep expressions!

Look just above the windows of the house. The Seymour family emblem (a pair of angel's wings) is carved above each one. Isn't that lovely?"

Getting there   National grid ref. SU975219
- Bus: number 1 to Petworth from Midhurst, Worthing, Pulborough and Storrington.
- Train: nearest station is Pulborough.
- Useful website: Petworth House and Park www.nationaltrust.org.uk, tel. 01793 343929.

ROTTINGDEAN

RUDYARD & ROCKPOOLS

Rottingdean is a pretty little village on the coast between Brighton and Saltdean, although at first glance it seems besieged by traffic. Look closer, however, and it has the ingredients for a varied and interesting day out. We divide our time in two, depending on the tide. When the tide is out there is much to enjoy on the beach. When the tide is in, we head towards the village set back a few hundred yards from the busy main coast road, and enjoy the atmosphere. Before you make the trip to Rottingdean, some readings from the *Just So Stories* would set the scene well, as their author, Rudyard Kipling (1865-1936), lived in the village from 1897 to 1902, and wrote many of his famous stories and poems here.

The Grange Art Gallery & Museum

In the heart of Rottingdean is a traditional village pond, and close by is The Grange. Downstairs is the local library, and upstairs is a quirky and personal museum, the sort my children love. A life-size figure of Rudyard Kipling, seated at his writing desk, quite makes you jump as you turn and see it. In fact, the last time we were there, two ladies came in and in hushed tones decided he was a real man sitting in his office whom they had better not disturb. We barely contained our giggles!

Behind 'Mr Kipling' is a small corner, furnished with cushions, to sit and read from a collection of his books, put there to be enjoyed by all.

A copy of his famous poem *If* hangs on the door, there are illustrations from stories which will be familiar, and details of his extraordinary and at times tragic life.

We were amazed to find that Rottingdean had a history of smuggling. There is a display called 'Inside the Smugglers' Tunnel': depicting white cliffs, with brandy flagons and chests of lace and finery and, of course, a lantern. It is said that almost everyone in the village was involved in the dark doings, including the wonderfully named Captain Dunk, village butcher and gang leader, and even the vicar! There is a poster dated October 19th 1782, offering £500.00, a huge amount then, as a reward for information about a smuggling ship sighted in the area.

Caves in the chalky cliffs were connected by tunnels to cellars under the houses and inns all the way up the High Street to the Green. Are they still there, we wonder? The gangs onshore used a 'spout lantern' to signal to the boats, called luggers. By moving a hand across the light, messages could be sent out to sea. Even the windmill up on Beacon Hill was used as a signalling device; if the sails were standing in one position they knew it was safe to land, if in another, they lurked out at sea. The mail coach was also deployed, the post horn playing one tune for 'all clear', another to say 'the excise men are coming!' The cunning smugglers even moved white chalk boulders, used to guide the excise officers safely along the cliff at night, to lead them straight over the edge!

There is much to satisfy the more bloodthirsty customer here, and to inspire games of piracy and adventure when back home. Also in this gallery small people can dress up as a Rottingdean resident of yester-year, and there is a hamper full of dolls and clothes you can dress them in, as well as dolls' houses to be gazed at and played with.

Gardens on the village green

After all that literary and historical stimulation, you might be ready for the delicious cakes served in the gardens of The Grange, in fine weather. Alternatively, you can find a perfect picnic spot in the nearby Kipling Gardens. These lovely gardens on the village green are set out like a series of rooms, leading one to another, inviting you to explore them.

If there are those in your party who love flowers, flint walls, perfect lawns and inspiring planting, they will be delighted. For those who prefer a game of hide-and-seek, it is a perfect venue. Send off those able to read to find a verse of Kipling's poem *Our England is a Garden* (on the wall of the gazebo), while you set out the picnic. If it is raining, or too sunny, sit in the little pavilion at the north-east corner of the garden and admire views up to Beacon Down and the magnificent smock mill built by Thomas Beard around 1802.

A short, bracing walk takes you up to the mill, with fantastic sea views. It ground corn for the village from 1802 to 1881. Young cricketers will be interested to learn that cricket was played on the adjacent field for many years, and on one occasion a mighty sweep sent the ball right down Hog Plat, and 67 runs were scored!

Rottingdean rockpools

To avoid disappointment, consult the tide tables and don't go down to the rocks in bad weather when the sea can be treacherous. Equipment really depends on what you feel like carrying. Some suggestions: buckets, nets (not necessarily big ones), a small pot or two, a grown-up's hand to hold on slippery rocks, a pocket guide to the seashore, a towel. The chalky cliffs on this stretch of coast extend out into the sea, giving the water its particular slightly milky quality. A lesson in coastal erosion can be delivered in the guise of having fun! The remains of the eroded cliffs now provide hours of rockpooling pleasure. However, rocks can be horribly slippery and scratchy. Bring plasters! The pools are often deeper than they look, and the tide can come in with surprising speed.

Some children prefer wellies, although once filled with water they can be pretty miserable. Gina preferred those jelly-like summer sandals but my son would always opt for old trainers and then perform daring leaps, much to my dismay!

It takes a few minutes to acclimatise your eyes to the magical world beneath the water surface that in a few hours' time will be hidden from view. Encourage children to creep up quietly and stare into the pool, as they are more likely to spot something if it hasn't been scared away.

Gently dip the net in, transfer the contents to your bucket for close observation then, equally gently, put them back in the pool.

Finding a comical hermit crab is usually the highlight of our day, and look out for seaweeds, crabs, starfish, anemones and tiny darting fish. Be careful of the velvet swimming crab though, as it can nip. Often the real treasure will be a pebble with a hole in it, or a tiny iridescent shell.

Time can seem to stand still for young and old alike, absorbed in observing a natural world and responding to cries of 'come and look, see what I've found!'

GINA SAYS

"It seems that everywhere we go in Sussex, tales of smugglers follow. Dark, intriguing stories pop up everywhere! Even the people you would least expect to have been involved often were, or at least it implies that in this poem by Rudyard Kipling, which is displayed in the museum."

SMUGGLERS SONG

If you wake at midnight to hear horse's feet,
Don't go drawing back the blind, or looking in the street.
Them that asks no questions isn't told a lie
Watch the wall my darling, while the Gentlemen go by!

Getting there   National grid ref. TQ368022

◉ Bus: 12, 12A and 13 from Brighton and Eastbourne; 14, 14A, from Brighton and Peacehaven; 27A from Brighton.

◉ The Grange Art Gallery & Museum, tel. 01273 301004.

ST LEONARD'S FOREST

DRAGONS & MUDLARKS

S t Leonard's Forest can be hard to find and we have never seen a signpost directing us here, but it is definitely worth searching out. Roost Hole car park is just off Hammerpond Road, on St Leonard's Road, on the left if you are coming from Horsham.

Although close to the busy centres of Crawley and Horsham, this special heathland forest has a mysterious and isolated air. There are many legends surrounding the forest. Also, St Leonard's Forest was used by smugglers, the trees providing hiding places for the contraband. Gruesome stories were probably spread by the smugglers to keep innocent folk away. One involved a headless horseman, Squire Poulet, who preyed on any lone riders venturing into the forest after dark. Another told of a smuggler named Mick Mills, who encountered the Devil and bet that he could outrun him. A long, straight forest track is still called 'Mick Mills' Race'

Of most thrilling interest to children, though, is the legend of the dragon, or worm, described in *The Legend of the Dragon of St Leonard's Forest*, a pamphlet printed by John Trundle in London in 1614:

> *Its long neck had a circle of white scales about it, along its back appeared to be blackish. The dragon had a very proud countenance and on hearing or seeing either man or cattle would raise its neck upright and seem to listen and look about, with great arrogance.*

Although able to kill both men and dogs with its venom, the dragon only ate rabbits. Before this report, legend spoke of St Leonard fighting with a 'mighty worm in the forest'. He encountered the dragon often, and repeatedly tried to slay it. During these many encounters drops of the saint's blood fell on the ground and there grew lilies-of-the-valley, which can still be seen each year. This exciting poem describes the action.

> By land he fought a dangerous worm
>> Of monstrous size, who for the term
> Of countless years consumed the land
>> With cries and fears of every hand.
> He'd slay both men and beast for food
>> For human flesh and oxen meat
> (No matter which) to him were sweet
>> Folks say that in the dreadful fight
> He pored his blood, but at the sight
>> Sweet lilies sprung out from the stain
> Which since have bloomed and bloomed again.

So, the dragon and saint legend was very firmly entrenched in the mythology of the forest, although there is no proof that St Leonard, who is the patron saint of pregnant women and prisoners of war (strange combination) ever visited Sussex. St Leonard also banished snakes from the forest, and silenced nightingales, who disturbed his prayers. However, both snakes and birds have been spotted since.

Muddy fun

An outing to St Leonard's Forest will give great pleasure to children who love mud, so prepare well beforehand, perhaps covering car seats with very old sheets or towels. Take lots of water, both to drink and wash hands. Wear clothes that really don't matter, and Wellington boots. Bring a bucket or two for mucking about in the streams. And don't forget a good book for you to read while they squelch about.

Tell stories about the dragon and perhaps read of other dragons. Both my children were absolutely gripped by C.S. Lewis's *Narnia* books In

DRAGON MASK

It's great fun to charge around the forest pretending to be St Leonard's fierce dragon and a simple home-made mask can greatly add to the effect. Make them simple but sturdy as anything too flimsy will soon fall apart under robust outdoor conditions. Recycled cardboard boxes are perfect.

1. Cut out a cardboard shield shape the approximate size of your child's face.

2. Make sure the eye holes are on the big side as a restricted view can be dangerous, especially outdoors. If this proves difficult cut out a letter box-like slit that accommodates both eyes as this is much better for visibility.

3. Attach string or ribbons to either side at about ear level for tying on securely. Once the mask fits comfortably, your child can decorate his or her own mask as wildly as they like.

For a more elaborate effect, tie paper bows to a long 'spine' or 'tail' of strong string, and fix it to the centre of the mask top. These make great shapes as the child rushes about, and adds general dragon-ness.

The Voyage of the Dawn Treader a particularly unpleasant boy, name of Eustace, is turned into a dragon. Read this chapter out loud to your children, and the rest of the books, too. It might be fun to make a dragon or two before you go. Squashed eggboxes give a good crusty surface to cut out and paint, with red eyes and curling paper flames. These can be used as props for role play games, with stick swords found *in situ* for slaying!

Finding the mud

There are many streams in the forest. We leave the car park on a steep path by a sign telling the dragon legend, and how the forest was described as 'a vast and unfrequented place, full of unwholesome shades and overgrown hollows where this serpent is thought to breed'. GULP! This describes the beast as 9 foot (3 metres) or more in length with a red tummy.

Hopefully, deer and butterflies, and the odd friendly Labrador will be all you encounter on your visit. Follow the path and very soon you come to a green and gloomy dell; take the right fork to a bridge across a stream. Clamber down and there is the mud! There are muddy

---

GLORIOUS MUD

When you get home, why not extend the muddy fun. You need: and old washing up bowl or old seed tray (without holes in the bottom), a quarter bag of cheap potting compost, old squeezy bottles filled with water, plastic toy dragons and dinosaurs, leaves, twigs and pebbles.

WHAT TO DO

• *Put the soil in the bowl.*
• *Squirt in water.*
• *Mix with twigs and hands.*
• *Add toys, leaves and pebbles.*
• *Squirt in more water.*

Have fun!

---

banks to climb, and slide down. There are branches and twigs to form dams and big sticks to breech them. Find somewhere to perch in comfort, and let the young dragon-hunters absorb themselves in play.

Try not to be horrified by the bloodthirsty yells and splashes. We are so keen to keep our children clean and safe, but remind yourself that this is a BIG ADVENTURE! So much can be learnt from playing with natural materials in fresh air, minds buzzing with myths and legends, and the opportunity to extend their experience of the world.

The forest is also wonderful for walking, so if your party consists of those too 'mature' for mudslides, there is much to see and enjoy. Robin Hood, though not from these parts, has often played a part in our woodland walks. A great place to ambush Maid Marian, or your sister!

GINA SAYS

"*My family have always loved visiting woods, and when I was really small we would march round them rather than stroll, imagining we were 'Dad's Army,' which I must have seen on TV. I was always 'Captain Marilyn' (Mainwaring!) and would make my brother be 'Pike' so I could order him about!*

Now sometimes it's just nice to get away from it all, and stomp in some mud. It's so invigorating!"

Getting there   National grid ref. TQ206298

◉ Bus: regular services to both Crawley and Horsham.
◉ Train: stations at both Crawley and Horsham.

TILGATE PARK

ANIMAL CRACKERS

There is so much to do and see at this very popular park, on the edge of Crawley. It is easy to get to and a welcome oasis in what is a busy town. Londoners can get here quite easily as well. It is great for everyone from preschoolers to grannies. We usually have three 'sections' to our visit: the Nature Centre, the children's play area and the park and lake.

In the car park (small charge) is a map of the whole park. It is probably a good idea to head straight for the play area. If the children spot it, they will whine until you go. Get it over with! Sit back and relax while they let off steam. Unless, that is, you have reckless tinies with you, in which case supervision will be needed, especially at busier times such as at weekends and school holidays.

When some energy has been expended, head towards the Nature Centre. You are nearly there when you see a large, green, metal sculpture of a lion, or Aslan, as we heard him being addressed. While the children climbed on him, our timid dog cowered, trembled and looked in the other direction! (Dogs are welcome in the park, but not the Nature Centre or play area.)

On entering the Nature Centre there is a 'jungly' feeling with lots of hanging foliage and raucous birdcalls. A small child in our group suggested singing 'Walking Through the Jungle' as we approached, so we did, with all the appropriate actions.

Walking through the jungle
What do you see?
Can you hear a noise?
What could it be?

This is a favourite preschool rhyme, and great fun to sing *in situ*, with actions, although the reply, 'A chicken looking for his tea' was somehow out of context!

There is much to see, and read, throughout the centre. There are extremely decorative ornamental hens pecking about, and large, grassy open runs for guinea pigs and rabbits. We were very impressed by a huge, red-wattled turkey, standing high above our heads atop an aviary, displaying his fabulous plumage and literally shaking his tail feathers. He had a prime view of everyone coming in and treated us all to a fine show. A keeper said they weren't sure how he got up or down, as no one had ever seen him do it! Gina pointed out that this living, breathing, haughty creature bore no resemblance to his poor cousins in the supermarket.

In the Discovery Room is a biodiversity display including a tank with local fish and another with a python curled up asleep. By lifting flaps there are interesting facts to be discovered, for instance did you know that sharks can smell one drop of blood in a million drops of water! Look up to see a life-size cut-out of a Californian condor spreading its huge wings over your head. There are sections on fish, amphibians, reptiles, birds and mammals, with a small piece showing the link from dinosaurs to our present-day birds. Displays show which creatures are becoming extinct and those already gone. Nearby, small children can come face to face with big hairy tarantulas, as their tanks are at child height. Great!

In the poultry area look out for the Polish chicken, which has a huge puffball of feathers on its tiny head. To Gina's delight there are goats (she wants one), peacocks and a white fluffy calf. New to Tilgate is a pair of otters, which feed at intervals throughout the day, and you can be sure to see them at these times. Otters are making a comeback, due to factors such as the cleaning up of our rivers, a ban on otter hunting, and the reintroduction of animals bred in captivity. What good news! Apparently otters spend 70 percent of every 24 hours asleep, just like a teenager I know!

We watched three very large pink pigs in their sty, sound asleep all in a row, snoring loudly. To everyone's amusement the middle pig, who turned out to be unmistakably the daddy, after sighing loudly and attempting to claim a bit more bed space, gave up and slowly tottered out, grunting, to have a prolonged wallow in his bath. He drew quite a crowd. The sows continued to snooze, waffling and squirming, deep in piggy dreams.

There are so many creatures to see, including deer, turtles, beautiful red squirrels, handsome White Park cattle, sheep and owls and, depending on the time of year, piglets, chicks and other baby animals. Taps are provided for handwashing after your visit .

The park & lakes

The park was once part of a much larger estate. The three lakes were probably constructed in medieval times to serve the iron industry. The largest lake was used by Sir Malcom Campbell in the 1930s and 1940 to test and develop his famous speedboat *Bluebird*. The Walled Garden, which once served as the kitchen garden for the Tilgate Estate, is beautifully maintained. There are picnic tables, some under cover, and a café. There is also a small maze, in which I was soon lost and had to be rescued by the more maze-savvy younger members of the family.

The park is marvellous for ball games, frisbee and general larking about. It stretches down to a huge lake, ideal for floating model boats. A pleasant walk takes you right round the lake's perimeter, giving lovely views of the trees reflected in the water, and an opportunity to spot dragonflies, toads and frogs and, of course, many birds, including swans and ducks. All three British species of woodpecker can be seen here. Listen out for the tapping, and that odd laughing call, or 'yaffle', of the green woodpecker.

We always return to say hello to the giant redwood tree in the park, below the inn on a path to the right. It is huge, and it's fun to try and measure its girth, either in footsteps round the base, or outstretched arms around the trunk. There is also an interesting wooden sculpture nearby, depicting five types of leaves.

There are many lovely spots to set up your picnic, with trees to climb and space to run. It always amazes me that although it is so close to busy roads and large towns, Tilgate Park gives us a real feeling of escape from the whirl of 'things to be done'.

Buchan Country Park

Only 2 miles (3 km) from Crawley there is another great place to explore, Buchan Country Park. Sculptures of owls, fish and deer are dotted through the park, and are fun to find. The park is a combination of woodland and heathland. There is a countryside centre (open on Sunday afternoons), toilets and a car park, but no café. Many paths, being hard surfaced, are accessible even in the rain. Bluebells are a wonderful sight in spring, and look out for dragonflies, and butterflies, in this 'site of nature conservation'.

GINA SAYS

"We watched some massive pink pigs in the Nature Centre for ages, they were so funny! Also I had no idea how many different types of chicken there are! I really want a baby goat, and I think it would be lovely to have a little pig too. So I was thrilled to find that you can actually adopt a Tilgate animal! If you do, it will still be kept at the Nature Centre, but your name will be displayed as its adoptive parent. I am definitely asking for a pig for my birthday! The rest of the park was also lovely, a great place for big family picnics."

Getting there   National grid ref. TQ275345

◗ Train to Crawley or Three Bridges then a bus to Tilgate shops, followed by a ten-minute walk to the park.

◗ Useful websites: Tilgate Park: www.crawley.gov.uk, tel 01293 521168. Buchan Country Park: www.westsussex.gov.uk, tel. 01293 542088.

WEST WITTERING

LIFE'S A BEACH

This is a lovely beach setting for our last old-fashioned day out, suitable for all the family to enjoy perfect fine sand and sparkling sea. A day to spend engrossed in the timeless and absorbing pleasures of digging, building and dreaming.

This delightful sandy beach is situated 7 miles (11 km) out of Chichester on the A286. There are signpopsts to West Wittering Beach. The West Wittering Estate has preserved the area from development and the beach holds Blue Flag and the Solent Water Quality Award.

There are several shops in West Wittering village where you can buy any emergency buckets and other supplies. Neighbouring East Wittering has banks and other amenities. There is easy parking directly behind the beach and the car park, for which you will need change, costs between £1 and £7 depending on the season and time of day.

Before you set off from home, collect a selection of small, inexpensive prizes: non-sticky sweets, stickers, hair clips, toy animals, dinosaurs, a bucket and spade for each child, bat, balls and a frisbee. The day before, to build up excitement, recruit the children to make their own sandcastle flags with lolly sticks, paper and glue. Decorate with bright felt pens: fairies, skull and crossbones, batman signs, whatever takes their fancy.

To avoid arriving with the adults cross and festooned with towels, cameras, coolboxes, toddlers and tears, we find those large, lightweight laundry bags extremely useful. They can be carried by willing helpers for short distances and, depending on the size of the party, one can contain swimsuits, goggles, waterwings, etc, another holds towels (the more the better), beach mats and picnic blankets. All sand toys together too. It is a good idea to assemble this the day before, including the prizes, flags and, of course, the picnic.

Drive along behind the beach. Once through the car park you will find three toilet blocks and the younger your children are, the nearer to these you may wish to park. Two of the blocks have freshwater shower facilities, very useful at the end of the day, and most helpfully, there are taps providing drinking water to replenish your water bottles at intervals along the road.

There are pathways at frequent intervals between the car park and the beach, so you won't have a long trek. At this point our family all have different ideas about where to set up base camp – near the life-guards, close to the ice-cream shop and so on, but usually when a decision is made and the blankets spread, the grumbles subside and everyone is more or less happy.

Sand sculpting

Choose a landmark, such as a numbered groyne, beach hut or landmark nearby and point it out to all members of the party – grown ups can get lost too. I can well remember my panic as a child coming back from the water's edge and seeing what appeared to be hundreds of identical mums on deckchairs – which one was mine? – and snivelling until she came to claim me.

Hand out the buckets and send the children off to collect as many interesting beach treasures as possible. We find that further along the beach there seem to be more shells, sticks, feathers and bits of weed. When the treasure seekers return, suggest a list of possible sand sculptures they could make: a mermaid; a speed boat (to sit in); a dinosaur; a cake; a dolphin or a shark; a giant sea horse; a castle. (Tip: to give your castle an authentic gothic look, shape the turrets into points and then carefully drip seawater over them to give a melting, decaying Gaudi-esque quality.)

CRAB SANDWICHES

For a beach picnic, there is nothing like crab sandwiches for a taste of the sea.

* *sliced wholemeal bread, buttered*
* *a dressed crab*
* *1 tbsp mayonnaise*
* *black pepper*
* *freshly squeezed lemon juice*
* *cucumber, sliced really thin*

1. In a bowl combine the crab meat, mayonnaise, lemon juice and black pepper.

2. Spread thinly on slices of bread, add the cucumber slices and sandwich together.

3. Cut into triangles, wrap in greaseproof paper or non-PVC wrap and pack in rigid containers. Keep in a cool box.

Empty the buckets of treasures and use them, along with the home-made flags, to decorate the sculptures and remember to take photos of them with the proud artists alongside.

Then it will probably be time for the crab sandwiches and lunch, before judging can commence, with due ceremony. Taking time the judge can stroll around, noting each sculpture from every angle, finding a particular aspect of each one that stands out and can be commended. (Acting skills are useful here.) Everyone can be a winner and categories can be tailored to fit your competitors: the most beautiful, gruesome, imaginative, humorous, detailed, etc., or whatever is most appropriate.

Time to award those prizes!

Water games

The sea here seems to be fairly shallow for some distance so can be ideal for games of frisbee and water polo. There are lifeguards on duty in the summer months to consult about the tides and sea conditions.

Or you could try Neptune's Kingdom. We love this game, it's ideal for five or more able swimmers. One person is Neptune and everyone else are merpeople. Neptune can, with a touch, turn the merpeople to stone. There they must stand, legs apart and arms stretched out, till released from the spell by a fellow merperson swimming through their legs or under their arms. The game can go on until everyone has been petrified or Neptune is exhausted and throws in his trident.

Races are fun especially if a spectator has a stopwatch and doesn't mind being splashed. To add to the fun, produce small treats at intervals to act as diversions and consolation prizes.

For young children the sea can be overwhelming but holding a grown-up's or big sister's or brother's hand and jumping over the tiny waves at the edge is tremendous fun and a great confidence booster. Just filling and emptying buckets can also be very absorbing.

When the tide goes out, a wide expanse of flat sand is revealed, which is perfect for cricket, rounders, frisbee, beach football or cricket, or practising dance moves.

GINA SAYS

"The beach is really absolutely lovely. The sea is completely clean and clear and there's not a drop of oil to be seen and as an added bonus the sand is just right for burying your brother.

I always like bringing a book with me to the beach because it is incredibly relaxing to read while listening to the waves washing up and down the shore. Also, as long as you know where the family base is, and your parents are OK with it, there is plenty to explore just walking from one end of the beach to another. Remember also to take balls and bats, which can save the day in almost any situation."

Getting there   National grid ref. SZ769981

❯ Bus: 52 and 53 from Chichester bus station.
  The nearest stop is the Old House at Home pub and the beach is ten minutes walk.
❯ Train: nearest station is Chichester.
❯ The Salterns Way cycle and wheelchair path run from the centre of Chichester to the
  West Wittering beach car park, but it is a long way to push a wheel chair.
❯ Useful website: www.westwitteringbeach.co.uk

OTHER PLACES TO VISIT

All the days out in this book are designed to be free, or at least as cheap as possible, apart from transport costs, so that everyone can enjoy them without having to worry about their budget. Most of them, however, are within easy reach of a larger attraction for which you have to pay. You may have a little bit extra in the kitty, or be a member of the National Trust, and so can get in free to castles and stately homes, or be eligible for group discounts, or have train tickets that combine with free entry, and it would be a shame to miss out. Below are listed, in chapter order, some of the more interesting places to visit, with contact details and website addresses, so you can check out your destination before you go and combine your old-fashioned cost-free day out with a paid-for treat.

Ashdown Forest
See the lovely llamas and alpacas at The Llama Park.
www.llamapark.co.uk
Telephone 01825 712040

Balcombe Viaduct
Very near to Balcombe is the ever popular Ardingly Reservoir. To continue the railway theme you could also go to the beautifully restored Bluebell Railway.
www.bluebell-railway.co.uk
Telephone 01825 720825

Beachy Head
Fort Fun is not only a great place for running off excess energy but also has an indoor soft area

should the weather turns nasty.
See also Cuckmere Haven.
www.fortfun.co.uk
Telephone 01323 642833

Brighton
The Sealife Centre never fails to fascinate and the pier is always fun, although you can soon rack up the pounds with rides and arcade.
A ride along the seafront on Volk's Electric Railway is always a treat.
www.sealifeeurope.com
Telephone 01273 604234
www.brightonpier.co.uk
Telephone 01273 609361
www.volkselectricrailway.co.uk
Telephone 01273 292718

Camber Sands

Venture over the border to Dungeness in Kent and take a ride on the delightful Romney, Hythe and Dymchurch Railway. Built in 1927 as the 'World's Smallest Public Railway' it provides a riveting journey through time.
www.rhdr.org.uk
Telephone 01797 362353

Chanctonbury Ring

For the energetic, a bracing walk up to the Iron-Age fort on Cissbury Hill will be rewarded by fabulous views of the county that stretch away to Selsey Bill.
www.findon.info

Cuckmere Haven

Alfriston boasts the very first National Trust property ever acquired, Alfriston Clergy House. Further along the A259 towards Eastbourne is the Seven Sisters Sheep Centre at East Dean, especially good at lambing time.
www.nationaltrust.org.uk
Telephone 01323 870001
www.sheepcentre.co.uk
Telephone 01323 423302

Cuckoo Trail

At Horam, near Heathfield, is the Sussex Farm Museum and near the Polegate end of the trail is Drusillas Park with its lovely zoo.
www.sussexmuseums.co.uk
Telephone 01435 812597
www.drusillas.co.uk
Telephone 01323 874100

Devil's Dyke

Although only open Sundays and Bank Holidays throughout the summer, West Blatchington Mill is always worth a trip.
www.blatchington.virtualmuseum.info
Telephone 01273 776017

Friston Forest

The nearby Seeven Sisters Country Park Visitor Centre at Exceat is full of useful information and further down the coast, the Seaford Museum is well worth a visit. Housed in a Martello Tower, its displays include a dressmaker's parlour, the contents of a toy, chemist and photographer's shop, along with a Victorian schoolroom.
www.seafordmuseum.co.uk
Telephone 01323 898222

Hastings

Continue the sea theme at Underwater World. More history can be absorbed while charging around the grounds of Hastings Castle and the 1066 Story.
www.underwaterworld-hastings.co.uk
Telephone 01424 718776
www.discoverhastings.co.uk

Highdown Hill

At Littlehampton's Look and Sea Visitor Centre you get a great 360 degree panorama of the county from the Viewing Tower.
www.lookandsea.co.uk
Telephone 01903 718984

Horsham Museum & St Leonard's Forest

Leonardslee Gardens can be found at nearby Turner's Hill. Along with acres of wonderful gardens and lakes there are the added attractions of wandering wallabies, vintage motor cars and an exhibition of dolls' houses.
www.leonardslee.com
Telephone 01403 891212

Hove

A culture-fest can always be had by a visit to the Royal Pavilion at Brighton. The Pavilion is a great source for oriental-style projects to be made later at home.
See also Brighton.
www.royalpavilion.org.uk
Telephone 01273 290900

Pett Level

An absorbing couple of hours can easily be passed in Rye Museum. Full of shore-related exhibits about shipwrecks, invasion and smugglers. It also houses a great collection of the idiosyncratic Rye Pottery, including the famous Sussex Pig.
www.ryemuseum.co.uk
Telephone 01797 226728

Petworth

Just a stone's throw from the grandeur of Petworth Park is the humble but charming Petworth Cottage Museum. Mrs Cumming's Cottage can be found at 346 High Street and presents a restored worker's cottage just as it would have been in the 1910s.
www.petworthcottagemuseum.co.uk
Telephone 01798 342100

Rottingdean

Back along the A259 coast road towards Brighton, is the ever popular Roedean Café and Miniature Golf Course.
Telephone 01273 570513
In the other direction lies the glamorous Art Deco Lido at Saltdean for bracing outdoor swimming in spring and summer.
Telephone 01273 888308

Tilgate Park

Tulley's Maze Fun Park at Turner's Hill boasts a maze created from that American favourite, maize (sweet corn to you and me).
www.tulleysmaizemaze.co.uk
Telephone 01342 718472

West Wittering

Chichester has some really good indoor venues such as Chichester Cathedral and the newly renovated Pallant House. Fishbourne Roman Palace is only a few miles away.
www.chichestercathedral.org.uk
Telephone 01243 782595
www.pallant.org.uk
Telephone 01243 774557
www.sussexpast.co.uk
Telephone 01243 785859

INDEX